Surviving
on
Broken Pieces

S. Renee Brown

ISBN 978-1-64258-480-6 (paperback)
ISBN 978-1-64258-481-3 (digital)

Copyright © 2018 by S. Renee Brown

All rights reserved. No part of this publication may be reproduced, distributed, or transmitted in any form or by any means, including photocopying, recording, or other electronic or mechanical methods without the prior written permission of the publisher. For permission requests, solicit the publisher via the address below.

Christian Faith Publishing, Inc.
832 Park Avenue
Meadville, PA 16335
www.christianfaithpublishing.com

Printed in the United States of America

Acknowledgment

First and foremost, all Glory is given to God. He has been the one holding me up when all I wanted to do was lie down.

To the incredible women of God in my life—Mae, Stephanie, Shajuanna, and the women in our prayer group and Bible study—I say thank you. Each of you have touched my life in so many amazing ways. You all have shown me what walking in holiness is really about. I thank you, God, for great examples of women who not only speak the word but live the word. Amen.

To my family, I love you and God loves you too. I especially want to say thank you to my nieces and nephews from the oldest to youngest. To those of you in my family who may feel left out, or less fortunate because your accomplishments hasn't been as great as other family members. I want you to know that if you believe in God and believe in yourself no goal is impossible to reach. Those of you who seem to struggle with who you are and how you fit into God's perfect plan, I love you all. Those of you who have struggled as well as those of you who seem to never struggle, I want you all to know that all things are possible through God.

God is always there even when you think he is not. Pick yourself up, dust yourself off, cry out to God, and He will hear you and deliver you out of the mess you may find yourself in.

There is much purging that must be done in our lives because we have allowed the enemy, Satan, to have control of our mind and body. Everything that I have shared about my past to the present has been a process. I gradually gave the enemy control, and it has since been a process of allowing God to gain total control. Romans 12:28 (NLT) reads, "Don't copy the behavior and customs of this world but let God transform you into a new person by changing the way you think. Then you will learn to know God's will for your life which is good, pleasing and perfect."

The enemy is out to destroy you at any cost. Satan has no love for you. You must stop letting the things and people of this world control you. Stop letting things or people be your focal point.

Allow the love of Jesus Christ to reign in your heart and in your mind. Reach out to God. He will, in turn, reach out to you. Once you ask Jesus into your heart, there is nothing he won't do for you.

God will change you; he changed me. I'm no longer bound by other people's opinion of me and no longer bound by my own negative thoughts about myself. *I am free!* Free from all the hurt, self-inflicted pain, and suffering of my past, and that's what I want for you all. I strive daily to keep this mind and body subjected to the things of Christ. It is said best in Philippians 3:13–14 (NLT): "No dear brothers and sisters I have not achieved it but I focus on this one thing forgetting the past and looking forward to what lies ahead. I press on to reach the end of the race and receive the heavenly prize for which God through Christ Jesus is calling us." There is something greater for you! I love you all. My prayer is that you will allow God to open your eyes so that you can see the greatness that I see in you.

Be blessed. I love you! Know that your aunt survived on broken pieces and you can too! Life is not always pleasant, but God will always be there.

Chapter 1

The Pains of Life

Shutting myself off was always easier than facing the pain—the unbearable feeling of my heart being crushed, the excruciating pain of past failures, and disappointment, the deep sobs that come in the night when everything is still and quiet and I can't help but remember the things that have happened in my life that made me close myself off. I had put a Do Not Disturb sign on the door. The lyrics of the of the failures and disappointment were playing over and over like a broken record. Everything is so unclear. How did I get here?

As I listened to the thoughts, I began to open my heart's wounds and began to truly feel the pain of love gone wrong, the pain of past rejections and abandonment as I buried myself deeper and deeper in the pillow of tears. I asked this question during those nights: why did these things happen to me? And yet the question remains unanswered.

Finally, daylight. The crying stops for a moment, and I am able to push the pain aside. The memories of the hurt are pushed to the far corner of my mind only because I have refused to deal with it.

Now, I have added another layer of brick to that wall of pain. Soon, very soon, that wall will encapsulate me and become my hiding place from the world. That wall will be my escape from the pain of childhood problems, marriage gone bad, sibling rivalry, lying family, untrustworthy friends, and personal losses, the past hurts that caused me to close myself off.

Once I have built that wall and basically shut myself off from the world, what will happen next? The depression would set in and the mind battles would begin. The loud voice in my head would get busy telling me, "Don't get out of bed this morning. If you get up, you'll have to think, function, and rehash the pain of yesterday. You don't want to remember, you don't want to feel any emotions." There were days when I didn't want to open the blinds, I didn't want to answer the phone, and I didn't want to see anyone. I wanted it all to go away. All I really wanted was to sit in the darkness of my mind alone, trying to get through the daytime hours and pray silently that nightfall will come a little earlier so that I will be in my comfort zone of darkness, self-pity, and gloom.

Depression is an emotional trap set by Satan himself. This trap is hard to shake, and most of the time, we are tied up in it and we don't want to shake it because it gives us a hiding place from our hurt and ourselves. Depression will take you on a roller-coaster ride: up and down, high and low. And for me, when the ride would seemingly be coming to an end, I still could not get off. Why? Because I had not come to grips with the root of the problem.

As I look back, I have to admit that some of the problems were myself and my distorted thinking. We are all human, and in that, we need love and affection and security to be made to feel safe and accepted by others. When these things don't happen, we sometimes feel worthless, we think we have failed somehow because we can't fix what is alienating us, and we withdraw into our own little world.

As I continued to ponder on things, I began to ask myself, *Why not just end it all? Why not just put myself out of the misery and pain of it all? It's just too much. It's too hard to keep up this pretense another day. I'm tired of fighting a losing battle. There is no light at the end of this tunnel, only more of the same.* I kept saying to myself that everything is not worth it. I want to end it.

Then out of nowhere, there was this soft voice I could hear so quietly within myself, saying, "NO! That's not the answer. I know that you are hurting. I feel your pain. I see everything that you are going through." I knew that it was the soft voice of Jesus I had heard so much about. I began to sit still and listen, and I felt his presence so intensely within me. He said, "I can help you. I can heal you. I can ease the pain, take away the hurt, guilt, and anger." He said, "I love you! I want to come into your life and show you how to live again." By then, I was sobbing, with my face drenched with tears because I could feel Jesus's love for me and I need to feel loved.

Those may not be the exact words that Jesus is saying to you, but he is speaking words to your heart. Just listen and you will hear him.

It is not God's will for us to live a depressed life. If you can believe in Him, your life will change. If you will believe that Jesus died and rose again, read Romans 10:9–10 (KJV): "That if thou shalt confess with thy mouth The Lord Jesus and shalt believe in thine heart that God hath raised him from the dead thou shalt be saved. For with the heart man believe unto righteousness and with the mouth confession is made unto salvation." Speak it out of your mouth, ask God to forgive your sins and come into your heart; he will. Once you have invited him in, you will feel the warmth of his love and the power of His presence.

You will begin, as I began, to slowly kick down those bricks of isolation and seclusion. Then as the last brick falls, you will step out victorious over your circumstances. You will begin to see that life is new again. Your life will begin to have meaning; your life will have purpose. You will ask yourself, *Is this real? Is this really me?* The answer will be yes because God is a healer, God is a deliverer, God is a fixer of the heart, and he will renew your mind and your way of thinking. God will give you a new attitude so that you can get to the altitude he created you for. It is written in Isaiah 40:31, "But those who trust in the Lord will find new strength. They will soar high on wings like eagles. They will walk and not faint." God will help those who believe in him. How do I know? Because he did it for me and he will do it for you. God loves us all. He is not a respecter of persons. He does not show favoritism. He will do for you what he has done for me if you confess and believe. Get in his word, read and know God's promises for yourself, let him transform you by renewing your mind.

I survived on broken pieces.

Chapter 2

The Journey

Life is a journey. As we plot the course of our lives, we plan to go from point A to point B in order to reach our destination.

We think that getting from A to B will be smooth sailing, but as we continue on course, we find that the wind can change directions and the seas become rough. And some of us become shipwrecked. In order to continue, we have to survive on broken pieces. I too became shipwrecked. I saw pieces of my life, my future, and my plans floating all around me. Although at that time the picture of my life was a dull image of what I had hope for, I still had to grab what was in front of me and come in on broken pieces. The pieces that we reach for may be weakened themselves by the waters of life. They may be tattered and frail, but upon them rests a glimmer of hope. At some point in our lives, hope is all we need to help us survive on broken pieces. That glimmer of hope for me was that faith spoken of in the word of God in Matthew 17:20: "If you have faith as a grain of mustard seed." I had that small, minute sense of faith that if I just stay the course, don't give up, don't give in, and don't give out, I will one day come into my place of destiny, my place of purpose, and my place of peace. Understand that none of this has been easy. I was surviving on broken pieces.

The hard knocks of life, as we sometimes call them. These blows were not delivered to go down for the count but rather that we examine where we are.

We are to get back up and fight. Fight the good fight of faith and finish the course even if like me, you have to come in on broken pieces.

The word of God in Jeremiah 29:11-12 For I know the plans I have for you," declares the Lord," plans to prosper you and not harm you, plans to give you a hope and a future. Then you will call upon me and go pray to me and I will listen to you." Once we have been broken, we have already been knocked to our knees. Why not just stay where we are and pray? God said he will listen. "You will seek me and find me when you search for me with all your heart" (Jer. 29:13).

Cry out to God. He already knows but he wants you to acknowledge your brokenness, hurt, disappointment, sense of failure. When you do that, God says this: "'I will be found by you,' says that Lord 'and will bring you back from captivity. Jeremiah 29:14. You have been held captive by the battles in your mind, by the enemy (Satan).'" He (satan) use situations and circumstances of your life to keep you down. The word lets us know that God will come and get you and deliver you out of the hands of the enemy.

God will take you out of the terrible situation you are going through. Why? Because he has a plan and a purpose for your life. God wants to bring you back to him where you belong.

It may not look like it now, you may not be able to wrap your mind around the concept of it, but if you will only trust God, he will take you places you never imagine. But before any of this can take place, you must accept his son Jesus Christ as Lord and savior over your life. John 3:16 (KJV) says, "For God so loved the world that *he gave his* only begotten son, that whosoever believeth in him should not perish but have everlasting Life." Romans 10:9–10 says, "That if thou shall confess with thy mouth the Lord Jesus and shalt believe in thine heart that God hath raised him from the dead thou shalt be saved. For with the heart man believe unto righteous and with the mouth congression is made unto salvation." So I say to you, believe and confess then trust God. Believe his words and obey his commandments.

Chapter 3

Life

Life is something that sometimes, most times, takes many of us by surprise. No matter how you may plan your course or plot your journey, life always throws us a curve ball. There is no navigation system, no turn-by-turn instructions.

You can be the most prepared person God ever created, but life will still happen.

I have a wonderful friend. She's a true friend. She's slender and proportioned nicely, and it is hard for her to understand how some women seem to let their bodies go and become so overweight and out of shape. Well, I'm not a size 10, and sometimes it can be a bit frustrating as I listen to her. She doesn't discriminate with just size it's hair, clothing, shoes anything that stands out to her she has a comment, but I am going to stick to size because that's a topic I'm well acquainted with.

Whenever she sees an overweight person and asks, "I wonder how she got that fat?" I reply, "Life. We are not all alike. We may be male or female, but that is where the line is drawn. Life affects everyone differently. How we handle life's situation is different for each of us."

Take stress, for instance. Some people like my friend who has gone through a stressful experience in her life and she couldn't eat food made her sick, therefore her size 10 turned into a size 6. As for me, stress took me in the opposite direction because food became my best friend.

SURVIVING ON BROKEN PIECES

When our lives are altered, so is our ability to function "normally" because nobody can really define *normal*. They may attempt to define *abnormal*, but all of it is just man's opinion.

There is no roadmap to life. If we had one, we could handle stress easier and we could make distinguished plans and stick to them. If we had a roadmap to life, I would know that I will get married and in five years my husband will leave me, and I can make plans for that and be ready when it happens. If we had a roadmap to life, I would know my child at age ten will have a terminal disease; I will know how to handle that. If we had a roadmap to life, I would know that my job will downsize after ten years of employment and I will be dismissed, so I won't buy that new house. I'll make sure all my bills are paid because the roadmap to life has told me I will need to reinvent myself for a new career.

There is no roadmap to life; that's why it takes us by surprise.

The only sure thing we know about life is we are born and we will die, but what happens in between, we don't know. There are no other certainties of life outside of the fact that we live.

How we live is what's important. We should live joyous, peaceful lives.

In the last few years, I have begun to live a more fulfilled and happy life because of Jesus Christ, my Lord and savior.

He is the roadmap of life. I had stressed myself to the max, but I still was trying to keep pushing. More bills than money, marriage on the rocks, distanced from my family, overweight and to add more stress a bad report from the doctor.

All of the diagnosis given to me by the doctor were all due to stress. When I did my research, stress was the most common denominator. I couldn't believe this was happening to me.

I cried and cried after that. I had a reality check. I did this to myself by allowing the stress of life to take control of my life. I gave in to it; I allowed it to go to work with me every day, come home with me every day, live in me every day.

God heard my cries, my prayers for help, and he knows I was sincere. I repented to God for allowing something outside of him to be in control of my life, my thoughts, my emotions. I know I keep on repeating this, but God has a plan and a purpose for our lives; I said our lives, not our demise.

Don't continue to head down that path of destruction when you feel down and out, when you feel life has given you a raw deal. Call on Jesus! He will hear your cry, and he will come to your rescue. Because he heard me, I am now learning to be stress free by casting my cares on him. I don't carry these things that are too heavy for me; I give them over to Jesus. The word of God lets me know in Isaiah 53:4–6 (KJV). "Surely he hath borne our griefs, and carried our sorrows: yet we did not esteem him stricken, smitten of God, afflicted VS. 5 But he was wounded for our transgressions, he was bruised for our iniquities, the chastisement of our peace was upon him and with his stripes we are healed. VS.6 All we like sheep have gone astray; we have turned every one to his own way; and the Lord hath laid on him the iniquity of us all."

Jesus went through the pain, the agony, the stress, the sorrows. And when I came to grips with that, when I actually got that word in my heart and believed it, that was when my life began to change. That's when I realized there is a roadmap for our lives. God has it, and if we will follow His plan for our lives, it will be all right. I didn't say you won't encounter issues; life still happens. But God says, "I am with you even unto the end of the world" (Matt. 28:20, KJV). The word also lets me know that if God is for me who can be against me. We have to give our lives to him in order for him to be the triumphant one in our lives, to be Lord.

My doctor's report is much better I've lost weight my lab reports are good, It's because of my Lord and Savior Jesus Christ that I survived on broken pieces. I gave all my cares and concerns to him!

Chapter 4

My Broken Marriage Turned into Blessings

Many of us today go through the hurt and pain of a broken marriage. It is devastating for some, and many of us don't recover. Others pretend to but never really recover. We can move on, but the wounds are still there. Some of us turn to vices that are unhealthy for us, such as alcohol, drugs, sex, gambling, gossiping, and being in other people's business. Pain knows no boundaries, and we want to numb the pain—at least I did. Although I did not turn to the vices above, I had my own personal demons to deal with. We only want to be free from all the things that came with being broken. I lived with that pain and loneliness for many years.

It took a while, but I woke up and realized that my husband and I weren't as close as we had been early on in our marriage. We basically, throughout the majority of our years together, were divided, but I had blinders on and couldn't or didn't see it. The word of God tells us that a house divided cannot stand, and divided we fell.

We were two different people from the start, but I thought I could fit him into my world. And before we married, I had put myself halfway in his. I went into the marriage with unrealistic ideas. We were different; we wanted two different things. For a while, I compromised with myself and who I was to fit into his world to try to make him happy. The word of God also says that in order for two to walk together, to unite together, they must agree. We didn't agree on much, and we seldom agreed on the things that mattered.

For me, what mattered was living for God and doing what is pleasing to God, but he wasn't interested with things pertaining to God. Over the course of our last two years together, things grew worse. There was no fighting or arguments; it was basically silent in the house. We didn't sleep in the same room; he moved out of our bedroom. We became strangers who shared a house. He cooked his food; I cooked mine. He washed his clothes; I washed mine. We were divided in every sense of the word. Our marriage was failing. When he comes home, I go into my bedroom. We didn't even share any common space together. We were divided. If I walked down the hall and he was at the hall closet, he would hug the door to prevent me from touching him. It was heartbreaking to see him pull so far away from me. After months of not talking and not touching, I finally told him that I will move out as soon as I get some bills paid off and free up money to get a place to live in. I got no response at all—total silence. I expected an argument, a debate, a quick conversation, but there was only silence. I finished washing dishes and went back to my room hurt and disappointed. I hoped that he would say, "I don't want you to leave. Let's try to work it out. But nothing.

My faith in God was strong, but I still couldn't understand why this was happening to me. I prayed and cried many nights, but I kept assuring myself that God will work it out. No matter how bad things got for me, I never stopped praying. I even asked God to change me if he wasn't going to change my husband.

I didn't want to go through another failed marriage. It took years for me to get over the first one, and now it was happening again. How that crushed my self-esteem. It made me feel worthless; I was a failure again. I would have to deal with shame again, with people gossiping about me again. Those things I prayed about over and over in my mind.

Fighting through tears, fighting through brokenness, disappointment, and heartache, I still would get the strength I needed to pray. I know that without prayer, without faith, I would not survive.

For months, I gradually packed boxes and put them in the dining room we didn't use. It was in plain sight, hoping for some kind of response. I hoped he would see I was serious and would ask me to stay. He never asked.

What happened next was, God began to give me peace as I continued to pray. My room had become the only place I was comfortable in in the house. I was like a stranger in my own house. I dreaded going home after work knowing he would be there, knowing the loneliness that I felt because of the distance between us. Our house at one time was warm and inviting; now, it only felt cold and empty. This was a stressful way to live.

I continued to work toward paying off bills, but I felt that because of the financial situation I was in, I might have to live stressed and depressed. But faith kicked in, and I began to tell God how I trust him and if he didn't make a way for me to get out of the situation, then I would endure what I had to endure. I released it all to God—everything—because I was doing all I could and things were no better.

But God! Is all I can say. I am in a prayer group that meets on Saturday morning. That morning, I was seated by a window and could hear noise from outside I looked out and saw a moving truck. The people across the street were moving at that time it was of no significance to me but later it all became very clear.

I'm going to go back for a moment to say that God has put three great women of God in my life. And one of them is a true prophetess of God, meaning when God speaks through her, he brings it to pass. So over a period of time, God had spoken through her. I would be moving, but God did not reveal when or how he was going to make this possible. But I believed and trusted God. After prayer, the prophetess and another friend and I went over to see what was going on. My friend started to ask questions about the house. She then told the lady who owned the house that I was looking for a house. The lady and I exchanged numbers, but she said she wasn't sure what she was going to do with the house. After she left, we started rejoicing, but reality set in just as quick as praise started. Doubt kicked in. Doubt told me I have no money for rent, deposit, or any money to have utilities turned on or moving expense. Just as quickly, faith kicked in and I began to thank God who told me it was going to all work out. And it did.

God set in order a remarkable chain of events in which I received a nice check from an unforeseen source. That check was enough for everything I needed and then some. Yes, God touched the lady's heart, and I got the house.

I had to come to grip with the fact that my marriage was over. I had everything packed and boxed up, and had moved them from the house to a storage facility believing God would make a way.

Still, my husband didn't say a thing. I wanted him to say something about my leaving, but his only response was silence. Even though God had said I was going to move, part of me still wanted to stay. Realistically, I knew God knew what was best for me, and I prayed and ask God to release my husband from me, I needed God to strengthen me so that I could let him go.

God had spoken through the prophetess that he would take care of me. God blessed me with the finances I needed. And as I said above, he also made it to where there was only one deposit required on all the utilities that had been turned on. I got new furniture. The house was updated, cleaned, ready, and better than the one I moved out of. I have not wanted anything else. I have not had anything shut off, reposed, or otherwise. God has done much more than I could have asked for. What I thought was a bad situation, God worked it all out for my good. God worked it all out for my good. I praise God because of what he has done for me. I learned through life situations. With God, nothing is impossible. I know from my personal experience that I tried to hold on to the very thing God wanted me to let go of. When I let go of what I didn't need, God blessed me with what I needed. I have peace, joy, and happiness.

I survived on broken pieces.

Chapter 5

Starved for Love and Neglected
A Letter to my Ex-Husband

I wanted so much to stay true to those wedding vows. I loved you, I respected you, and I was careful not to say anything demeaning toward you. I supported you in the things you desired to do, yet you never did those things for me.

You were not careful of my feelings. You never stood up for me, and you never praised me for any of my accomplishments. I always felt you despised me for wanting to better myself. I could look at you and see disgust and sometimes evil in your eyes toward me, yet silently, I kept going inwardly longing so much to have you by my side loving, and supporting me.

I was a love-starved, neglected woman and wife. You never really looked at me with warm, loving eyes. You showed no real affection toward me, no loving tender touches, no passionate kisses, not even a kiss on the cheek once in a while.

There was no laughter in our home, barely any communication, and no discussion of future plans. So to be honest; we had no future. I can see that so plainly now.

You didn't have any dreams of your own to share, no ambitions. You didn't aspire to do anything better for yourself. Where you were in life was all right for you as you had expressed on many occasions.

I wanted more—better—not just for me but for us. I didn't want finances to be a problem between us. So I worked two to three jobs because I wanted us to be able to go on vacations, weekend excursions, and long drives to explore places and experience new things. I wanted any opportunity to spend quality time with you. I felt love starved and neglected.

I often thought, even after the separation, *What did I do to make you so bitter toward me?* But as time went on, I realized I could not make you love me or treat me any differently than you did. I know that each person is accountable for their own actions, and no matter what I tried or how hard I tried, it just wasn't in you to appreciate me. It wasn't in you to celebrate me, nor was it in you to celebrate with me. How I wanted you by my side sharing in me and me sharing in you. We were supposed to be one, but that didn't happen.

I remember so vividly when you were expecting your first grandchild, a girl. I was sooo excited! I went all out and bought so many beautiful things for her. This was going to be one thing I know we could share in together, and being together was all I wanted.

Before the baby shower, you brought home a bag of hand-me-down clothes for the baby from a coworker. Nice clothing, but you wouldn't even spend your money on anything new. Nevertheless, I wanted you to look good so I washed and ironed every little piece of clothing so they would look nice and fresh.

Because I wanted you to feel proud, I took all the new things I brought, put them in nice gift bags, put your name on them, and you took them to a baby shower I was not asked to attend or take part in planning. Your family took total control of that. I felt so excluded, so isolated, not to mention the pain I felt that day as you walked out of the house and went to the shower alone. That day cut deep into my heart.

The pain and disappointment didn't stop there; it continued into our love life. Needless to say, it was in the toilet as well. I remember as if it were yesterday the last time I came on to you. Your response time was extremely slow, and you were very aggressive during the act as if you were punishing me for bothering you. But I was love starved and neglected.

For years, I thought this was how it's going to be, but things changed when I found Viagra and Cialis in your drawer. There had been no intimacy between us for months, not by my choice but by your own. It didn't take a rocket scientist to let me know you were in love with someone else. Wow! I didn't see that coming. I was truly blindsided due to the fact that I was love starved and neglected.

In my mind, I would have done anything to make it right, but in reality, I would have turned into someone whom I would have despised when I looked in the mirror.

I still stayed for months after that. I waited and I wanted his love and affection, but it never came. As time passed, I could see disgust, anger, and even hatred in his eyes. We never talked. He went his way and I went mine. I would stay in my room praying, hoping, wondering, trying to figure it out. *Why me? What's wrong with me. How did it come to this?* I was love starved and neglected.

One day, after fifteen months of emotional abuse, God Almighty helped me get my own place and I moved. It was bittersweet, but it was for my own good.

God in his mercy had everything so graciously and strategically planned for me until I needed nothing except answers as to how I ended up this way.

My emotions were still tied to my ex-husband. I wanted to know why, but there were no answers to that question. I was still feeling love starved and neglected.

For months, I was battling that thought in my mind and worrying. It was as if the ifs and the whys were taking control. Until one day, I decided I had to let it all go. I had made up in my mind to let it go before the thoughts of something I could not change took me to an early grave.

I had come to the knowledge that even in this, even in my hurt pain and despair, God still has a plan for me. And his plan is to help me prosper and bring me to his expected end, not mine. I turned it all over to God. He said in his word that I should cast my cares on him because he cares for the things that concern me.

Although I had been love starved and neglected for so, so many years of my marriage, I realized as some time passed that it started long before I got married. It started as a child, and I carried that feeling of being love starved and neglected with me. Many of my actions and reactions stemmed from the feelings of not having the love and attention I desired and felt I needed.

There is truth to that middle child syndrome; at least it was for me. I was between the baby and a sister older than me. We were the last of eleven children. The baby girl was the one to get plenty of love and attention. My sister before me is smart and pretty, so she got adoration also. But I was left feeling alone and undesired. I never seemed to do anything right. I was too fat, too clumsy, too this, too that. I became determined to find love and often in the wrong faces. My relationships were mostly physical, nothing real, nothing worth holding on to. But in my mind, for however long it was real, I continued to tell myself those relations had to mean something otherwise I would again find myself being love starved and neglected. Many of my actions left me in fear; but I was still hoping, praying, wishing for that one person who would love me for me—not compare me, not use me, not abuse me physically or emotionally.

However many, many years went by, I found him one day, and I realized he had been waiting for me. He was God; it was my Lord and Savior Jesus Christ whom I had found. He had been there all the time, waiting for me patiently with open arms. He held me ever so tightly. I felt the presence of his love so strong around me that it was as though he was truly holding me.

On his shoulder I cried, in his arms I cried. As the tears flowed, I could feel myself being cleansed—all the negative emotions, all the hurt, the pains, and the scars of the past were beginning to leave me—and in return I felt strengthened, assured, and hopeful for the first time in years. I felt alive, truly alive. The dark void was gone. I was set free—no longer love starved and neglected.

I am loved by my Heavenly Father, the one who will never leave me nor forsake me. He will always be in my cheering section, cheering me on to greater accomplishments. So my advice to you is, if you are or have been love starved and neglected, turn your life over to Jesus and you will survive on broken pieces.

I have!

Sometimes when we are love starved and feel neglected, we stay in situations far too long, most times out of fear of the unknown. It is easier to stay in the familiar. The signs are there telling us to move on, but we are afraid as I was. I felt helpless and hopeless because of my need to feel loved.

There comes a time when you have to realize your own self-worth and move on. Don't get comfortable in a situation, a relationship that is sucking you dry. Always remember God has something better for you. Believe in God and believe in yourself.

I survived on broken pieces

Chapter 6

Reflections

I grew up in a pretty close-knit community during a time when family meant something. Mothers and fathers were together in the home, they pulled together to keep strong family values.

Now these leaders are no longer alive, and family values especially the love in some families are not what it used to be.

Somehow as adults, we seem to forget the relationship we had with our siblings growing up. We forget the laughter, the warm summer night spent listening to the radio, outside late evening catching fireflies, and the enjoyment we had by just playing with each other. The days when everyone in that small community helped raise your children. Those days of love and respect.

I've seen the desire for control, greed, and lust for material things and money destroy even the closest families, leaving behind sadness, devastation, pain, bitterness, and unforgivingness.

I think back to a Saturday afternoon. It was a funeral of the dad of a childhood friend, a pillar of our community. I remember the look of hurt, pain, and sadness in her eyes. It was a look I had seen in my own reflection some years before. It was a look of devastation, confusion, and unbelief to say the least.

Her eyes expressed the helplessness of a family being torn apart. This family was close growing up. When you see one of them there was always two or three more not far behind.

The look in her eyes was saying, *Why has this happened to my family? Why are we so distant?* She then spoke, "We are here to bury our dad, and we can't come together for that."

How did we arrive here, drifted apart from each other? We thought we would always be close, but something is missing. It's love, the love we shared as children growing up. How can we teach our children and show them the value of family when we don't seem to believe in it anymore ourselves? It's that to-each-his-own mentality that has creeped in. I see the selfishness, the unforgivingness, lies, greed that has torn us apart.

I watched as one of her brother sat restlessly through the service. I thought it was the anxiety of losing a loved one, and I'm certain some of it was. I listened as others talked about how the brothers must pull together, how they are now the leaders. The more I listened, I thought to myself that something is wrong. One of the brothers didn't attend the service, and he lived in that town. Not seeing that brother, I was certain in my heart that what I saw on my friend's face was unmistakably true. Hurt can only be briefly masked; it can never be totally covered.

When I saw my friend at the cemetery, no words were needed to be exchanged. I could see the hurt in her eyes as she began to say, "I wish things could be the way they were when we were growing up. Why is life so complicated?" as I looked at the tears well in her eyes. She went on to say, "I wish I could feel that love again, experience that laughter and just the simple joy of family. Now it is so much confusion, so much anger. This one not talking to that one, and the family as a unit is crumbling."

As I listened to her, I could see that this family, like so many others including my own, needed forgiveness: forgiveness from each other in order to move on to begin to love and live again, forgiveness from God to help them heal.

What is being accomplished by holding on to old grudges? Others have gone on with their lives while you are still expelling useless energy majoring in minor things. Valuable time is being lost with people we love because of pride and unforgivingness. It's time to stop wasting time being stuck on stupid things. When all is said and done, if you don't try to fix it, you'll be left along with a life of grudges and regrets. You'll be bitter at others because you chose to live apart from them.

Don't allow petty things to tear your family and your friendships apart. Don't be stagnated. Let it go and move on. Take the lifeline that's being thrown to you. Forgive; haven't you wasted enough time? I beg you to go and get it right with that brother, sister, or friend, and then get it right with God.

Colossians 3:13 (NIV) says, "Bear with each other and forgive what ever! grievances you may have against one another. Forgive as the Lord forgave you." God forgave us by choice; we must also forgive by choice. Holding a grudge only hurts those who refuse to forgive. Think about those who are up at night, who are angry or emotional when a certain name is mentioned, whose life has been disrupted because they will not let it go, whose health is going down because of the stress of it all. That's the person holding a grudge. Some may say, "None of that is happening to me." Maybe not, but I know you are slowly dying inside; I was. Holding on to these things gave me no comfort, no peace.

We are not a perfect people; we all make mistakes. Through God's love, it is possible to forgive. And once you do that, you will be able to heal. Once you heal, you will make new and better memories to share with the ones you love. When you release that old stuff, you get your joy back, you smile, you laugh, you live, you love; it's that simple. Reconnect with the ones you love.

Surviving on broken pieces.

Chapter 7

Innocence Shattered
Who It Made Me Become

I was ten years old and still having a normal childhood as far as I can recall. While sitting on the sofa watching TV covered up with a blanket, one of the neighborhood guys came over and sat next to me. I thought nothing of it. He came over to our house regularly. He was one of the guys who played basketball with my brother. No need to think anything bad was going to happen; I was ten.

Where I grew up, people trusted people. And now I know some people who shouldn't have been trusted. Every time this guy came over, he would come in the house and sit beside me and talk a little and watch TV. Then eventually, he got under the covers with me, just sitting and watching TV. He was grooming me.

As time passed, he would take my hand and rub it across the front of his pants. I felt like that wasn't right, but I didn't know what to do. I was scared and too scared to tell. I don't remember if he threatened me; I just remember being scared. As time passed, he finally took it out of his pants and put his hand over mine and rubbed up and down. My hand would feel wet and sticky. This happened a few times and then it stopped. He never touched me, but he made me touch him many times over. It was a frightening experience for a ten-year-old. Up to this day, I never learned why he picked me to do that to.

Another incident happened to me when I was between eleven and twelve years of age. I and about eight other girls were in an after-school activity club lead by an older woman, about sixty, in our community. After our meetings, she would always take us home. This particular evening, she asked her husband to take us home. She was a teacher and had some schoolwork to do. I was the last one to be dropped off on the drive home. This old man, about sixty years old, offered me fifty cents if I would let him touch me in the off-limits area. As soon as he put the car in park I opened the door and jumped out of his car scared and nervous. I was too scared to tell my parents; I feared they would not believe me. This was a grown man and I was a child. Even then, I was sure they would have thought I did something wrong. Because that was what I thought, I never told anyone until I was grown. Needless to say, I quit going to these meetings. No one ever asked why. I would have been too ashamed to tell them the truth anyway. I don't know why these men picked me to try to fulfill their sick desires. I'm just grateful nothing more than that happen at that time.

As I got older, worse things did happen to me. I was raped as a teenager by a cousin. I was seventeen at that time and was staying for a week with a cousin. We had been out with some of her friends. She was older than me, but our families were pretty close, especially our mothers. After we got home, she showed me where I would be sleeping and I went to bed. I woke up from a sound sleep because I felt something; someone was actually trying to and actually did penetrate me before I could fight the attacker off. I was still dazed from drinking and wasn't sure at first if it was happening for real or in a dream. Because he had also had too much to drink, it wasn't that hard to fight him off.

The next day, I left and again never told anyone about that incident. I was devastated because he was a relative, but later in life, I realized that a lot of rapes occur by family. It is not a good feeling having something like that happen it leaves a ton of emotional scars. By the time I was nineteen, I was date-raped, and there was no fighting this one off. I told him no, but he wouldn't stop. He basically told me I asked for it because I agreed to go to his house. It took years for me to come to grips with the fact that it wasn't my fault. And I constantly recall that memory from age ten up to now. The image of rape played the most. I was ashamed, but who could I tell? I knew I would have a label on me. In fact, I wondered why these things happened to me. Was I wearing an invisible sign that only sick-minded people could see?

Being a victim, and that's what I was because I didn't speak out, it made me feel dirty, worthless, and no good. I labeled myself because of the negative things that kept playing in my head.

I wanted love, marriage, all the good things that most young ladies dream about, but I felt that because of all that had happened to me, I was not worthy. So my life turned. I felt I was no longer a good girl; my identity was no longer the same.

I began to have boyfriends who would use me because I felt as if I didn't deserve any better and couldn't do anything better. My confidence was shattered, and it led me down a long and winding road, one that I'm not proud of but that's where I was. I was no dummy, but I acted like one and I allowed myself to be treated like one.

When a nice good guy, someone seemingly respectable, would approach me, I would treat him coldly. I always thought people knew as I knew that I was damaged goods, and he probably only wanted one thing from me and then he would drop me like a hot potato. I wasn't going to take that chance. If I was going to be hurt, it would be by my own doing, and of course that happened.

Because my self-worth and self-image were so low, I never felt pretty enough, good enough, or worthy enough for a good guy to come into my life. I was automatically attracted to the wrong guys. I felt most comfortable with the guy others thought was ugly or poor, the guy no one else wanted. Somehow, in my distorted brain, I felt choosing those guys made me feel better about myself.

I carried around so much guilt and so much shame for the kind of life I lived, and it wasn't living, only existing most days. I felt I had no life in me. I felt I had to settle for whoever would settle for me. I tried to keep up appearances even when I was with those guys. I was proud as if they were the cream of the crop. I had to believe it myself so others wouldn't see my pain. The one person I couldn't fool was myself. I had to look at myself in the mirror each day. I had to see myself after I had slept with these guys. I pretended to be someone I wasn't. I didn't like at all what I saw most days.

It wasn't until years later, after accepting Jesus in my life, that I was able to forgive myself for being raped and misused and for thinking so little of my own self. I had to forgive myself for using others for my own selfish actions.

I needed to be in control of something or someone because for so long, the things that happened in my life had controlled me. Lack of control in our lives can make us do some foolish things, things that are totally out of character. Lack of control for whatever reason can make us go against the true nature of who we really are and become someone we don't even know.

That's why I had to forgive myself, and if you have had any of these problems or other issues that had you acting against who you know as you, let it go. If you don't put your past behind you, it will hunt you for the rest of your life.

If someone somehow shattered your innocence, raped you, or abused you in some way, know that you have to let it go in order to gain your control back and live.

God wants us to live an abundant life. Not all abundance is wealth and money; but it is peace, love, joy, and happiness. And in order to have these things, you must have control of who you are.

You are not a label that you or someone else placed on you, you are not what happened to you.

In order for you to know who you are, you have to get to know Jesus as your Lord and Savior, and he will guide you into knowing just who he made you to be.

I survived on broken pieces.

Chapter 8

Who Am I?

This is a question I have asked myself for many years: Who am I?

Who is that person I see in the mirror each day? Who is she? Who is she supposed to become and how does she arrive there?

I didn't know her; I had no clue. All I know is that she is not the person she started out to become.

In my early years, I had dreams and ambitions, but they were short-lived. I was told from a fairly young age that I will never amount to anything. I was told that frequently, and it took root in my mind and in my heart. As years progressed, I was called crazy, no good, rotten, liar, and the list could go on and on.

For years, I listened to all those negative comments made by my family and so-called friends. Even people who didn't know me but just knew of me would comment as well.

This made it almost impossible for me to stay focused on the real me and not on what was being said to me and about me. My life took a downward spiral because of the negativity that had been planted in my mind. I didn't totally spiral out of control. I still had a partial sense of the person I truly wanted to be. Although as years passed, my dreams for myself seemed to get pushed further and further back, and at some point, I felt as if my life was useless. Every dream, every ambition seemed to fade away and I become less visible day by day.

I began to wear a mask because I didn't want anyone to know who I was, and at times, I didn't know who I was. I knew who I wanted to be, but because of all the negativity that had been instilled in me, I was a far cry from her.

When I was with my family, I wore one mask; with my friends, another; and in church yet another mask.

The masks were there to hide my true feelings; no one could know how fragile I really was. If they did, I think they would pick me like a dog does a bone. I was weak, but I had to wear a mask of strength and emotionally insecure but wore a mask of confidence. I had to somehow survive the madness in my life.

A lot of my hurt came from people close to me, and that left me insecure within myself. My family and friends would talk about me as if I wouldn't hear all the negative things they said.

Someone is always all too happy to rain on your parade via call, text, e-mail, or Facebook. The negative will be told. I had to learn some of those people who call themselves my friends were not and I also had to learn that many of those same people who said they love me didn't. Some people just want to get close to you to find out your weakness, your vulnerability, so their flaws won't be so easily seen. I had to learn the hard way: Don't let everyone in. It's okay to keep people at a distance. People don't have to know the intimate details of your life. Understand this: a lot of times, what they don't know, they will make up, and what you tell them, they will add to it. As for me, I'd rather let those types of people use their imagination because at least I know the truth, and when it is all said and done, the truth will prevail.

It took me a while to get to that point to accept the lies and hold my head up and smile with confidence knowing that someone was thinking enough of me to be their topic of conversation. Be it truth or lies, I was on someone's mind. I know to some it may not make sense, but I say as I've heard before, "Let your haters be your motivation."

We can't allow what others say about us to determine who we are. Instead, let it help take us to where we want to go. It's amazing to me that people invest time and energy into trying to make others look bad.

I look back at situations in my life that took such a great toll on me and really helped me to write this book.

There are so may incidents in my life that are very disturbing and some even devastating. As I look back, I know there was one person who really was out to destroy me. Of course I didn't see it as clearly as I do now. She was only being used by the enemy Satan. We can only be used by God or Satan. We can choose to serve only one master.

It's easy for someone to control you when you don't know who you are, when you don't know your self-worth. I didn't have a sense of belonging because of the years of being told I'll never be anything. I had no one to turn to, no one I could really trust or feel safe letting my guard down with. There was no one to talk to, so I isolated myself. That feeling of loneliness is indescribable: There is no one to laugh with, cry with, or talk to. It's just you alone with your thoughts and emotions, and that can send you into a very dark and dangerous place in your mind.

I often heard the rumors and lies about me; someone always made sure of that. But I tried never to let them see me hurt. I played it off like it was nothing. The mask was on, but I was breaking inside just a little bit more. It felt like someone had an ice pick and I was a block of ice being chipped away little by little. I was breaking off piece by piece. The pain was so intense. The anguish of it all was almost unbearable.

Lies can hurt so deeply, and the hurt continued to spill over for years of my life.

There was an incident I held on to for over twenty years due to a lie that was told. It was the Monday after the weekend of my tenth-year class reunion. I was at my parents' house when my brother came in the door and slapped me so hard. I looked around like, *Did that just happen to me?* I was in shock. My brother went on to tell me what someone else had told him. He immediately took their word as gospel truth and asked me nothing. He just took his and someone else's frustration out on me, and it all was a lie. Because of this, it severed the relationship between my brother and I and between a childhood friend and a close cousin. Lies tears people apart. It changes people's perceptions. I was truly devastated by this incident.

I eventually let that go. My cousin, who lives in another state, and I didn't communicate for many years. It wasn't until a family reunion in 2009 that I was able to get complete closure for myself. He and I finally talked. I was ready, and it wasn't so painful anymore. I needed him to know how I felt about it all in order to bring true closure to the incident in my life and forgive all involved. It was a hurtful lie and I allowed it to fester in my heart and cause myself undo pain for over twenty years.

Even as that situation was going on and coming to a close, there were other things happening as well. That same brother's wife had been telling lies and planting seeds of discord in the family. For whatever reason, she just hated me. I tried to figure out why, but I gave up. The lies, deceit, and manipulation had taken its toll on me. I isolated myself more and more. I didn't want to hear the latest gossip about me. Trying to stay by yourself doesn't work. People will take the time to find you when it involves your hurt. Somehow, some people tend to get pleasure from your pain.

I convinced myself that not being around family and friends or acquaintances was the only way I could keep what sanity I had left. When I went to family events, holiday dinners, birthday celebrations, I would be on pins and needles wondering who was going to whisper something to me that would cause me to be uncomfortable during the event. I was downright paranoid at times. When I could manage to make it through the event and get in my car, it was a sigh of relief. While driving home thoughts of who was talking about me were there in the back of my mind becoming louder and louder. I became extremely paranoid but still kept the mask on. No one could know what I was really feeling. I lived in a small town, and naturally, people talked. When my sister-in-law talked, people thought it was factual. But most of the time, she wasn't being truthful. I couldn't, wouldn't let people get close to me. I always felt like there was always a negative motive behind it. For so many times, because of the hurt and heartbreak, I wanted to tuck my tail and run. And many times I did. I made conversations short with acquaintances I may run into at a store. I had given someone too much control over my life.

I was a mess for so much of my adult life, and I didn't know what to do about it. I began to search myself. I began to think about the life or lack of life I was living. I knew I couldn't continue down this path; it was going to destroy me.

It was then that I started to remember the peace that I once had and all I could do was cry out to God. I was tired of being afraid, tired of living in fear of how people perceived me. I didn't want to spend my life isolated and empty. We are not meant to be alone; that's why God made Eve for Adam.

I cried out to God out of the affliction of my soul.

I wanted to get out of the snare that had been set for me. I wanted to be free from bondage. I wanted people to know the real me without the mask, the real me, not a picture someone else had painted.

I returned to church because that was the time I was at peace. I listened, I prayed, and God answered my prayer. He gave me peace, real peace. I was able to let go of all that negative stuff that had been planted in my mind. All the, lies deceit, discord, manipulation, hurt, anger, bitterness, unforgivingness, I let it go!

God let his love shine in me. I got my confidence back. I learned to love myself and those around me. I began to see myself as God sees me. He created me in his image, and everything God created is good and very good. The more I saw myself as a child of the king, a child of the most high, the true and living God, the more boldness I had. One day, I realized that it doesn't matter anymore what people say and think about me. What matters is what God says and thinks about me. The word of God lets me know in Romans 8:31 (AMP): "What shall we say to all these things – If God is for us who can be successful against us?" People are still taking, but guess what? I'm not listening. All I hear is the voice of my Lord saying, "Cast all your cares on me for I care for you." God wants us to come lay in the comfort of his word. Bask in the glory of his presence and have peace.

Now when I ask myself, who am I? My answer is I am who Gods say I am! And I know that all things are working for my own good.

I am surviving on broken pieces.

Chapter 9

Silent Cries

Sitting silently, my mind is racing with thought that come louder and louder. The cries of despair become stronger and stronger. I ask myself, *Why won't someone hear me?*

I am frantically crying out to you, can't you hear me? The emotional cries become deeper and deeper as I try to get your attention. Do you see me? Help me! Help me! I cry silently in my mind.

I can't speak of the pain. I feel the hurt goes too deep. If I tried to express myself, I would sob like a mad woman. If only you cared enough to open your heart, you would see. I say it every day with my eyes, the expression on my face, my posture. And if you would listen to my weak, broken voice, you would hear the inferiority and the desperation of wanting to be noticed, wanting to be helped.

The overwhelming pain still cuts deep. No one is listening to the cries of a person who only wants to be loved.

I need someone to talk to. I need someone to hear me. I need someone I can trust with all the mixed-up, pent-up emotions I am feeling. I'm trying to reach out for help, but no one will hear me. I feel as if I'm losing my mind. I toss and turn with thoughts of the past and present, and I wonder about a future.

Fear grips me. Panic soon follows. I have no one—no one. There is no one who will reach out to me. For years, this was me: crying out for someone, anyone, to notice that something was wrong. It wasn't anything that some real love, attention, and understanding wouldn't cure. No one took the time to just listen. They didn't care about my feelings. No one took time to hear my cries.

Why was I always talked about? Why was I considered a bad seed? I even wondered in the mist of all the turmoil: Was this really my family?

My sister could get beat down by her boyfriend, and the next day, my family was cool with the guy. I tried to rationalize how others could remain in their good graces, and I was an outcast. I watched as my family, one by one, walked away, never seeming to care about how I was feeling. Some of it was because they had been deceived. And oftentimes, we are, so that limits our ability to see things as they really are.

I continued to put up a good front when all the time I was building a fortress to keep everyone else out. I had encapsulated that hurt. This was my way of dealing with the anger that had built up in my life. I was angry because I felt alone, left out, and unloved. Isolation wasn't the best way to handle the situation, but what other choice did I have? At that time of hopelessness in my life, that seemed the only way.

Some people saw me as strong willed, a dominant person who's almost a rock because that's what I wanted them to see. I had an I-don't-care attitude. At times, that was another avenue I used to protect myself.

I was falling apart inside. I could never figure out why I wasn't loved, how others could remain in the family's good graces—but not me. Yes, I made mistakes. No, I'm not perfect, but none of us are. Others could get forgiveness, and everything was as if nothing ever happened. But not for me.

I know now that I had to be the fall guy. I was the one with the target on my back. For so many nights, I cried myself to sleep. I could never understand why I was hated so. If I was so bad, why didn't someone try to help fix me? Was it because it was much easier to point a finger and walk away?

Later, I thought no one wanted to get their hands dirty. Siding with me would mean going against the majority, and I was already the outcast. No one wanted to keep my company.

I went through years of separation anxiety. I still wanted and needed my family. I wanted their love and acceptance, but years passed and it never came.

One Sunday, I sat in church listening to the pastor preach on help for the hurting and power from your pain. Turning my pain into power intrigued me. As I sat up straight on the pew, I began to feel something through the words he spoke. Those words penetrated my heart. I began to feel a sense of peace all around me as the sermon continued. That peace was the presence of the spirit of God. I could feel his love all around me. It was as if He was saying, "I was misunderstood, I was forsaken, I was hated, but I endured it all for you." Tears began to flow down my cheeks. I felt such a comfort, such peace, and so much relief.

I could finally let go of years of pain and heartache, and know there is someone who could relate to how I felt.

God let me know that if I totally surrendered myself to him, he would heal my broken heart. He let me know he would heal me completely if I agreed to let it all go. I wanted to let go. I was tired of fighting to keep some form of normalcy in my life.

As I continued to sit with tears now streaming down my face, the pastor made an altar call. I moved quickly. I didn't look back to see who was getting up. I knew I was ready to release the past to let go of all the things that held me back, of all the weight that felt like tons. I couldn't move forward because the weight of my past was entirely too heavy.

As the pastor prayed, I could feel the love of God all around me. It was such a warmth, a rest, and a peaceful assurance that can't be explained. You have to experience it for yourself. I knew God loved me. I could hear Him sweetly, softly say, "Forgive, let it go, and heal." This for me was a rebirth, a new beginning, and a chance to live without restrictions from others. God assured me from that point that he would never leave me. Now I can boldly say as in Hebrews 13:6 (NKJV), "The Lord is my helper I will not fear. What can man do to me."

Now it doesn't matter what you may be going through. When circumstances seem too hard to bear, take the time to remember there is a God, the one and only who is standing right there waiting for you. His arms are outstretched. His heart pleading, "Let me in, allow me to heal you, allow me to pick up the pieces, allow me to love you."

Please let God in. He is knocking on the door of your heart. Let him in and begin to live again.

You're worth it.

I survived on broken pieces.

Chapter 10

Barren

In biblical days, women were frowned upon if they were not able to conceive. In today's society, that stigma can still be true. I have no children of my own, not by personal choice but by God's will, and I have accepted his will.

Now there were times when I blamed myself because of the things that happened in my life. I thought that not having children was a punishment from God, but I know that's not true.

My life was stressful even at age ten. I was diagnosed with what they called a nervous stomach. For months, I wasn't able to keep certain foods down, and many kinds of food had to be eliminated from my diet even then.

I internalize everything. I never talked about the things that really bothered me. I didn't know how to make myself heard without fear of feeling I would be misunderstood or judged.

It saddens me every time someone would ask me how many children I have. And when I reply that I have none, they would look at me like something is wrong with me. You would see eyebrows raised, and sometimes a mouth opens as if they may be gasping for air. Some of them would even have the indecency to ask why. That was the question that hurt the most. That one word cut so deep. When the conversation was over, I would walk away sad, hurt, and sometimes angry because I was childless and carrying guilt that it was all my fault.

Because I had not conceived in my early twenties, I figured I couldn't have children. So when people would ask, I would say I don't want any. That was my lie and I stuck to it. That lie became my Band-Aid. It covered up my true feelings, what I didn't want people to see.

I was now in my thirties and was reading over some scriptures from a Sunday service about our words being seed. The words we speak and continue to speak can spring up in our lives. Words are powerful, and they can be life changing. This caused me to think on some things. You know we always want to rationalize things. I remembered all the years I spoke I didn't want any children, when I actually did. I'm not saying that I actually spoke this into existence in my life, but I'm not saying I didn't either. What I am saying is that our words carry power. The Bible tell us in Proverbs 18:21, Amplified bible) "Death and life are in the power of the tongue. And those who love it and indulge it will eat its fruit and bear the consequences of their words."

So as I reflected back on my life, I can say for myself that because of the words that came out of my mouth, I had to bear unfavorable consequences behind my words. The words we speak, if we say them long enough, whether good or bad, they will take root and grow, and oftentimes we don't like what we planted. If we plant seeds of negativity, we get negative results. Do everything in your power to plant positive seed. Speak positive words over your life and the lives of others. Job 6:25 (KJV) says how forcible are right words. Can you see how what you say can bring positive or negative results? Matthew 12:37 For by the words thou shalt be justified and by thy words thou shalt be condemned." Again, we see the power of words. Speak words that can be justified by the word of God. You don't want your words to be condemning to yourself or others if you are a child of God.

As I talk about being barren of children understand that barrenness can also be a desolate, dry, unproductive area in your life. If that is the case, give these issues to God. He is the one who can give you living water. God can water your desert.

As I reflected back even more, I realized some things about myself. These thoughts came while I was in my forties. My life had been in such turmoil and disarray for so long that I was truly praising God I didn't have a child. I would have messed that baby up! It may have been like me: depressed and suffering from low self-esteem, anxiety, and oppression. That's to name only a few because that was what was inside of me during the earlier years of my life.

Although it hurts not to have a child, it hurts even worse when I think I could have had one and messed the child up to the point he/she could not have been productive in society.

I had serious issues, and when we don't face it, our children are always affected. They are affected by our emotions, our actions, and reactions.

I rely on and I'm grateful that God knows best. I think about my emotional state back then, I really couldn't have given a child a secure and positive home environment. I was too negative and down on myself for anything positive to happen outside of it being God's will.

I used to think my life would be so different with a child, but after truly searching, my heart and I came to the same conclusion: I would have loved the child, no doubt, with all that I was capable of, but until my emotions quit being all over the place, my child would have suffered needlessly by my hands. I know I could not have predicted the future for my child, but I know my future wasn't looking too bright at that time.

I've seen it happen: Mothers get upset because their boyfriends walked out on them, cheated on them. You are fighting and arguing all the time. Stop it! These things are leaving scars on your children. Your emotions become their hurt and frustration. I've seen it far more times than I care to speak about. I listened to a four-year-old child talk about killing her mom's boyfriend. She not only talked about killing him but what weapon she would use. This was because he kept physically abusing her mother.

Children are truly a gift from God; treat them that way. They are precious. They are truly loved by God. And God does not want them offended, abused, or hurt in any way.

Many women can be a mom, but don't forget to be a mother. Train your child, raise your child with values, show them love, show them how to live, and give them love. Encourage your child to be whatever they desire. Don't call them out of the name you gave them. Call them what you want to see them become. I just said words are a powerful tool. Use them to your advantage and to the advantage of your child.

I have been blessed enough over the years to surround myself with nieces and nephews for as long as I can remember. I have shared in their lives, triumphs, failures, and mishaps, and I have been blessed by it all.

Maybe you don't have any children of your own yet and it's possible that God doesn't have it on your list of accomplishments, but God never said we couldn't be part of that village to be instrumental in other children's lives.

So don't ever think just because you don't have children, you are incomplete. Not so!

We are complete in Christ. If you are in him, you are complete. God knows what he is doing at all times.

Being a mother isn't always about the number of children you birth. It's about the number of lives you touch.

I survive on broken pieces.

Chapter 11

Feeling Weak
A Talk with God and Myself.

Lord, help me not to fall back into needy feelings, the not-good-enough feelings, the feeling that I have to settle because I feel less than adequate.

You said I am fearfully and wonderfully made. Your words ring in my head. God and I are the majority; the greater one lives in me. You tell me to cast my cares on you because you care for me.

What am I feeling? Why do I feel this way? I feel like I am again trying to bring my past into my present and even my future.

Why? Because I feel lonely sometimes and he is comfort food to me. I am comfortable with him.

I already know there will never be a commitment. Is it really worth the emotional stress?

Am I really willing to go through this again just to have a male to talk to, to go places with, to flirt?

Have you forgotten in over thirty years he never totally committed to you or anyone else for that matter?

Do you really want to ride that emotional roller coaster again? Slap yourself, wake up; a reality check is needed here.

You are now content and have found a sense of happiness right where you are. Why rock the boat when you know it is only going to tip over again? And guess who will be drifting to shore alone—again?

It would be so easy to allow myself to fall for him again, but the real truth is I want God more than him.

If he were willing to make a commitment, would I really want that? So many factors to contend with. Would he commit to God and give up those worldly ways? I think not at this time.

Is he still good-time Charlie who just wants to show a girl a good time, make her wish it could last a life time, and then walk away? It is true in many instances that some things never change. This could very well lead me down a path I've been before and don't care to revisit.

The paths we take and the choices we make always end in consequences. What will be the end results of your choices?

Will they lead you down a path of peace, real love, joy, happiness or pain and heartache? Think long and hard and realistically before you make that choice. It may not be a choice you can quickly bounce back from.

There is only one choice when you are indecisive; that choice is do nothing, stand still, and wait on God. Allow God to direct your path. He tells us to wait, be encouraged, and he will strengthen us. We need strength when we are at the crossroads of life—go left or go right, God will give us the strength we need to survive on broken pieces.

Chapter 12

Feeling Weak

Wow! I am a little surprised that I find myself here again—vulnerable because of loneliness. I put myself in a backward situation. I looked back and I stepped back. I picked up a luggage from my past.

I said to myself, *This can't be happening again. God brought me out of bondage, and I will not return to the very thing that pulled me down emotionally. I have to take control!*

I feel sorry for a friend who has a long-distance relationship and the fellow doesn't want to commit. She is beside herself with worry, wondering if he's faithful.

I picked up that baggage from my past, and now I find myself wondering as she does. Seemingly, I know the answer. He always has two if not more women in his life at one time. I've found myself settling in hopes for years that one day he will choose me. After many years of an on-again-off-again relationship and a few words that came out of his mouth, I knew he would never commit to me and possibly not to any one woman.

Some years later, I received a phone call out of the blue it was him. My mind and my heart were elated because I had thought of him often, wondering if he married, how he was doing, or if he was well. It was great to hear his voice and know he was okay.

We met some weeks later. We had a great lunch and spent hours talking like we used to. We were to meet again, and the night before that, my cell phone went dead for no reason. The next morning, I called him after I got to work. As we talked, he seemed distant and vague. And then it hit me, was she there? Was another woman there?

That's when I knew for sure that I couldn't do this again. I cannot settle anymore. I remember him saying to me once that he didn't want to hurt the other woman he was seeing. But what he didn't say verbally, I read between the lines. He was saying it was all right to hurt me. Rejection is a hard pill to swallow.

After that call, I felt myself getting hurt all over again. And I knew I could not go back to the way I was and this could never go anywhere just like it didn't go anywhere all those years ago. I want more; I deserve more.

And my father in heaven has so much more in store for me, so I decided that day I will just wait!

My father is all I need right now. I know he is carrying me, and in his time, I will meet that right person. Until then, I may experience loneliness, but I'll never be alone.

What I must remember is that my God is with me always. I love my friend, but his love and loyalty is divided. God's love for me is pure and undivided.

I will no longer be a person in bondage to the feeling of being alone.

I do not have to settle.

Chapter 13

Temptation
It Will Lure, Entice, and Seduce

Temptation has destroyed many lives, relationships, and marriages. The temptation of the flesh has seduced and continues to seduce even the strongest of men and women.

Take Samson for example. He had to have Delilah. His flesh could not be satisfied until he had her, and look what happened: the very thing he burned in lust for deceived him and contributed to his demise. James 1:15 AMP. Says Then when the illicit desire has conceived it gives birth to sin; and when sin has run its course, it gives birth to death.

It may not be an instant death, but again, look at Samson. After his hair was cut, he lost his strength. Although we know strength didn't really lie in his hair, his strength came from his obedience to God. James 1:14 (amplified version) So elegantly puts it, "But each one is tempted when he is dragged away, enticed and baited(to commit sin) by his own (worldly) desire (lust, passion)

Samson was drawn away from God because of his own desire, his lust for Delilah. I didn't forget that God restored his strength in the end, but because of Samson's disobedience to God, I believe this is why he chose to die. He was remorseful for allowing himself to fall into that trap of temptation.

The eye wants what it sees and many times what it shouldn't have. Samson's eyes were taken out. He could no longer look upon the beauty of the things that enticed him the most. I think about the apostle Paul and what he wrote in 1 Corinthians 6:12 (KJV): "All things are lawful unto me but all things are not expedient, all things are lawful for me but, I will not be brought under the power of any." The same eyes that brought Samson under the power of the enemy were the very same eyes that were taken out. Ironic. He was blinded by lust with his sight and that same blinding lust left him without his sight. Now tell me that's not a trick of deception straight from Satan himself.

The pride of life can disguise itself in many ways. Samson showed pride and arrogance with his teases while under Delilah's spell. He knew no one could take his strength. Pride will make you laugh at things because you think you have the upper hand, as Samson did. It can make you look down on others, make you think you are smarter and better than others, but that very pride and arrogance can bring you to your knees.

Samson was untouchable for a time; but the seductive Delilah with her words smooth as butter, her mesmerizing tone alone, with her other luring factors, turned Samson, a man of extraordinary strength into powder, causing him to expose his weakness. James Chapter 1:12 (KJV) says, "Blessed is the man that endureth temptation." Samson didn't want to hold out; he didn't want to resist. It looked good, and pride had to have it. "Keep in mind pride goeth before destruction and a haughty spirit before a fall Proverbs 16:18, KJV). Being prideful and arrogant will cause you to stumble and fall. Watch your step!

Satan will tempt you by any means necessary. No one is exempt; he even tempted Jesus when he had come off a fast. Satan tempts us at vulnerable moments in our lives by using the lust of flesh, lust of eyes, and pride of life. He can only tempt us with the things we are drawn to, the things we like and enjoy. Satan is slick and cunning. Crafty and subtle, he has been using the same tricks for thousands of years, and guess what, they still work. He has no new tricks, only new people to use them on, and if truth be told, some of the same old people are still falling for his deceptive and treacherous ways.

He has had thousands of years to perfect his craft, and when you allow yourself to fall into temptation, believe me it will not end well for you. The odds are not in your favor no matter how things appear. Just remember that appearances change.

Yielding to temptation only brings bad news. It may look good, feel good, act good, taste good, smell good; but *wait* for it because the rug will be snatched from under you, the covers pulled off you, and you will be exposed!! You will be left trying to gather the broken pieces of your life.

The serpent tempted Eve in the garden as we know. His subtle tactics rendered her curious. His swag left her mesmerized, and she fell for it and fell from the grace of God. Not only did she fall, she took someone with her Adam, her husband.

When we are tempted, we often involve others because if truth be told, many of us don't want to go down that road alone so we give Satan two for one.

Temptation has broken up many homes, changed the course of many lives, and sent many people down a self-destructive path by planting seeds of deceit. I've heard this statement: "If God didn't want me to have it, he shouldn't have put that beauty of a woman before me and I wouldn't have committed adultery." God does not tempt any of us with wrongdoing!

Taking that money that doesn't belong to you and saying, if God had not given me this job I would not have been tempted to take the money. Temptation comes when you belittle and under mind someone to make yourself look good. It starts with a thought, then a lie. After that, deceit comes in.

Temptation appears to always have the better hand. That's because it is a deceiver and a destroyer. For that reason, we must resist temptation. It leads down a road of destruction and is a pathway to hell.

Many of us have seen what happens to people who have gotten caught up in various forms of temptation. They may have gotten forgiveness from God and maybe even the person or persons they hurt, but the damage done in so many cases is irreconcilable and lives are altered tremendously due to the mistakes of others. Please don't be deceived. Is it worth losing your family, your job, a good friend, or your soul to a burning hell? Don't be deceived! Many of us have walked down that twisted road of temptation. If truth be told, it leads us to nothing good. Although many of us try to do good, the evil of temptation is always there—waiting. We always have a choice. What will your choice be: to yield or not to yield? That is the question.

I am surviving on broken pieces.

Chapter 14

Sex Is Not Just a Physical Thing Satisfying the Body and What It Is Doing to Your Mind.

What happens after he has fulfilled his sexual desire and you're left empty and alone? Once the physical is over, the residue that it leaves on the mind can be toxic.

Once the encounter is over and he's gone or maybe he's still lying beside you, either way, you feel empty and alone. You lie there with tears streaming down your face wanting to be comforted, needing to be held to feel an emotional connection that isn't part of the physical act itself.

I wanted to hear the words "I love you" even if I knew he didn't mean it. For a brief moment, I thought, *If only he would whisper these words*. But they never came. Why? The answer is quite simple. His needs and desires have been fulfilled. It's over; he doesn't feel that connection any longer. There is no emotional tie and possibly never was. He doesn't need me until the next urge comes along. Who's to say that I mean anything more to him than just an avenue to satisfy his needs at that given moment? And the worst thing is that I probably already knew what the outcome would be.

The more I thought about it, the more I become angry, ashamed, and guilty. Angry because I knew better. I tried to cover the hurt of not being satisfied emotionally. He didn't say all the things I wanted to hear—needed to hear—in order to partially fill the void in my heart.

I felt ashamed because I allowed myself to be used yet another time. Then finally, the guilt. Why did I allow myself to go through this again? I felt worthless because that need to be validated wasn't met.

When you're in a relationship with someone, you are looking for commitment. We may say we're not, but if we are honest with ourselves, we are looking for someone to fill the emptiness in our lives. We are looking for someone to be comfortable with, laugh with, and share ourselves with.

Sex doesn't give us these things. Sex only satisfies the body. So what is it doing to your mind? When a man is trying to get his sexual needs met, he'll say all the things you want to hear: "I love you"; "I'm gonna be there for you"; "I won't ditch you like the last man"; "Baby, I wanna love all the pain away." We've heard these lines far too many times, but we have fallen for them over and over again.

There is no quick fix for years of feeling less. For some of us, we think sex is the cure-all answer; but it only complicates our thoughts and emotions, and adds to the feeling of inadequacy and leads some of us down a path of depression and even destruction. That's why the residue that sex leaves behind can be toxic.

We are full of "if only": If only the right man would come along. If only I could find someone who'll love me for me. If only I had someone who understands me, someone who can relate to what I need. If only continues to lead to I'm lonely. That void in our life, that hole in our heart still needs to be filled—for some of us, at any cost.

We at times compromise ourselves, knowing we are not the only woman in his life but we stupidly tell ourselves, *I'd rather have some of him than none of him.* How stupid is that?

We try to fool ourselves into thinking *It's okay to share him. It's okay if he abuses me because he loves me and he's jealous. It's okay if he's broke; I can take care of both of us. I just need him. It's just okay.*

Why do we try to convince ourselves to settle for less when we know that we need more, want more, desire more, and are worth so much more?

I know all too well the lengths that a woman will go to when she thinks that a man will make it all go away. Women, we give him too much credit. He can't always give you that emotional connection that you're looking for.

Sometimes, the emotional baggage we carry is a red flag with the words "Easy Target." We women sometimes appear desperate and overly eager to please. Some of us are easy prey because our war wounds are showing. We try to patch them over, but if someone looks hard enough, they see the drainage from the open wound that is hidden under the botched patchwork job. Your pain still shows to the keen, investigative eye.

Men can read some of us women like a fine novel; and let's face it, what they can't read, we are far too eager to tell. So they already know we are easy mark. Bull's eye.

He's already saying, "I can tap that easy target." All he has to do is play along, play it nice and slow, and ease right in.

I was that easy mark. I spent years searching for Mr. Right, only to find out later that he was Mr. Wrong again. Insanity is what I see when I look back at those experiences. I was doing the same thing the same way and expecting a different outcome. Why? How? I didn't change anything.

I met him, we talked, went on few dates. He made me comfortable enough to show him my wounds. Bam! In the bed, and soon it's over. He didn't want all that residue left by years of insecurity. He wasn't interested in helping me heal. He was only interested in getting his thrills. Once that was over, he moved on to the next easy prey leaving me feeling used yet again.

After years of the wrong men, I was finally introduced to the right man who turned my life around. He's the one who filled my void. He healed the hole in my heart. His name is Jesus the Christ. I found him to be loving, truthful, and my best friend, companion, and confidant. When he says "I love you," he meant it. He gave his life for me. He said he'll never leave me and he means it. I never have to look for him; he's always there. He never gets tired of me.

He was in my life at one time, but I left him, hoping to find another. He waited patiently for me to return; I did. I repented, expressed to him my sorrow for leaving him, and asked him to forgive me, and he took me back with open arms. He let me know that I set out searching for something that only he could give me. Jesus is the only one who can love the pain again. He says in his words "I will never leave you."

He won't use you and discard you. He loves us unconditionally, and isn't that what we need? Oh yes. And best of all, he won't lie; he can't lie.

When you decide to ask Jesus into your heart, ask him to forgive your sins and believe he has forgiven you. He will lead you in the way of truth and realness, and that's what we want. We want someone who is real, genuine, faithful, and attentive. Jesus is all that and more.

When you allow him to be your Lord and Savior, you will take on a new life, new characteristics. The old self as you know it will become new; you will begin to see things differently.

When we allow Jesus into our lives it is a choice to be better. We can continue to go down the path of emotional destruction or we can choose to allow God to be the man, the true man we have been searching for to comfort us. Allow him to lift up that bowed-down head, put a smile on your face, some pep in your step, and some sway in your hips. He can bring out a confidence in you that you never knew existed. I smile even as I write these words because that is just what he has done for me.

I was so heavy, so burdened, so broken, but now I'm changed. I'm no longer that person. I sing, I dance, I laugh, I live, and I love, all because of my risen Savior Jesus Christ. In him, I live. I live.

Invite him in. Let him know that you believe he lived, died for your sins, and rose. Ask him to forgive you and come into your heart.

Then and only then will you be able to understand what true love really is. Isn't it time for you to experience all the good things that God has waiting for you?

I am surviving on broken pieces.

Chapter 15

The Deceiver

Satan wants us to believe that God has not or will not forgive us. He wants us to think we have been too sinful, too bad, and have done too much to be forgiven. But not so!

In Isaiah 43:1 (AMP) The word says, "I have redeemed you, I have called you by name you are mine." It also tells us not to fear. Don't fear the lies that Satan is telling you. God says he has redeemed you. This means if you've asked him to forgive, you then you belong to him. The deceiver is a liar. He wants us to stay in bondage, to stay tied to sin. Isaiah 43:7(KJV) "Says" even everyone that is called by my name: for I have created him for my glory. If you have accepted Jesus as your Lord and savior you belong to God. Satan doesn't want you to know you were created for Gods glory. Satan doesn't want you to know that.

Think about it: You were created for God's glory. Almighty God took pleasure in creating you. He made you someone special.

The truth is, we don't always recognize the glory in ourselves because our mind is too cluttered. Our path may be like a wilderness and there is no clearing, no plain path to walk through.

God is a way maker. God will water your dry and thirsty soul, and he will go before you to make a plain path where there was none. We are precious in the sight of God. He loves us.

Since Adam and Eve, man has been fooled by Satan's tricks. He is the great deceiver. He is also called the accuser of men. He's nothing but a tattletale. He runs to God telling him about us and our shortcomings. Satan tries to magnify the wrong in our life as people of God.

He not only runs to God, but he plants seeds in our minds as well.

He is out to set a trap for you. Don't fall into it. Don't get tangled in it. When we are at our weakest point, at a vulnerable time in our lives, we may be discouraged because God hasn't answered our prayer or we lost a job, maybe didn't get the job we were praying about, our money is low, or we have a child in jail. Whatever weak moment in your life, Satan will take advantage of the opportunity to pounce all over you, to dribble you like a basketball.

The word of God tells us not to give place to the devil. Don't give him any space in your mind. None. Zero. Nada. If you give him any wiggle room, he is going to take your mind off who God is and magnify the problem. Once you start to concentrate on the problem instead of the one who has the solution, you are right where Satan wants you to be: rendered helpless and even at times hopeless. Then he really starts to work on our thoughts, and our thinking can get us so far offtrack.

We begin to analyze and rationalize the situation without realizing we have given Satan permission to mentally and physically drain us.

We start to question God: Why didn't you? How did you? Why did you? We want answers, and because things didn't turn out the way planned, we sometimes become angry with God. That's the wrong attitude to take, and that's where the deceiver wants us. He wants us at a place where we won't trust God. He wants us to think God has failed us, that God has let us down. The truth is, we allowed Satan to enter our thoughts and do what he does best—deceive.

Once the deception has taken place, it is hard sometimes to get back to the place we once were in God. The fight back to peace of mind becomes an all-out war. Satan does not want to give up. He will remind you that God wasn't there for you and will point out when.

We have to fight with all we have to get back on track, and even then, Satan continues to point his accusing finger at us trying to make us give up on God. *Don't do it!*

Satan wants to sell us a fantasy, a mirage, an illusion but God is a reality. Satan is a deceiver, but God is truth to every believer. Satan's mission in life is to have as many souls in hell with him as possible. He is not your friend; His job description is to kill, steal, and destroy by any means necessary.

Jesus came to give us life, not just mere existence. God wants us to live an abundant life filled with all the good things he has already provided.

If you find yourself veering off course, reset the compass of your mind and get back on track. God will forgive you; all you have to do is ask. Keep in mind that Satan is selling you a mirage. Nothing he tells you is the whole truth. Only Jesus is *the real thing*.

I know because I survived on broken pieces.

Chapter 16

Why Do You Kindle the Flames? You Never Meant to Stay

I asked myself why stir up old feelings that lead me down a path to nowhere? I asked him why kindle the flames when he knows he has no wood to keep the fire burning, and nothing is going to change.

He's taken me down this road before. It's the path that leads to nowhere, a sudden stop on a dead-end road.

In our past relationship, the decision had been made by him to turn around and go back every time. Go back to what? For him, it was what's familiar; for me that meant he didn't want anything in his life to change, that he didn't want a new adventure.

So again I ask him, *Why kindle the flames? Why do I allow him to come back into my life knowing that he hasn't changed? He still wants to remain carefree, living a life without limits without commitment.*

For so many years, the embers were there smoldering, and that one call from him started the kindling process all over again.

We had a friendship and a love affair like none I've ever known. The times that I spent with him made me believe it was possible to have the fairy tale, happy-ever-after story. Then of course reality had to rear its ugly head and let me know it is a fantasy: he is not your knight in shining armor; he will not rescue you.

What always amazed me was that my heart would still open to him in ways it never could with anyone else.

I believe my heart stayed connected to him because of the kindness he showed me over the years. When I was hurt, I could run to him. His kind, gentle words always uplifted me. He made me feel wonderful, He made me feel comfortable, and more than anything else, He made me feel loved. But at the end of the day, month, or year—however long it lasted—he could always walk away and seemingly never look back.

I know now, with our on-again-off-again relationship, that there was no chance of a lifelong commitment. Because he had been a part of my life for so long, I thought perhaps we might manage to be friends, but my problem was it was hard to separate my emotional ties with him and our friendship. I wanted what he could not give me, and that was himself. I wanted more of him than he were willing to give. I wanted the fantasy, and I found out he only wanted the intimacy.

I told him I had made a commitment to God and there could be no intimacy between us. The more we spent time together, I felt as though the intimacy was all he wanted. He was up for the challenge But he couldn't change my mind.

The flames were so easily kindled because of the memories I kept in my heart. No one ever measured up to him. For many years, no one ever could.

He knew how to treat me, what I liked, what I needed. He showed me respect. I never felt inadequate in any way when I was with him. He showed me love and taught me many of life's lessons.

With him, I knew happiness and heartbreak. He also let me know that the heart can't always have what it wants.

I had to take a step back and really take a clear look at the situation pondering old and new, unsure of what he really wanted from me outside of the physical. I soon became uncertain of what I wanted from him; too much time had passed. He had live too much of his life without me in it.

I was no longer that young girl who believed in fairy tales and happy ever after. I'm a mature woman who has faced many of life's challenges, and by the grace of God, I am still here. Every time he left me, a piece of me was broken, hurt, and in pain. I had to push hard to survive through the brokenness.

I don't know why, after years, he decided to call. For a brief moment, I thought, *Could he be ready to settle down?* I quickly shook off that thought. I knew in my heart I need to take control of my emotions. As I did this, I felt a sense of peace. I told myself not to rush and not to think too much. Don't plan the wedding and honeymoon just yet. Our minds can take us there when that flame has been kindled. I waited. I did nothing but let everything play out as it should.

Well, it played out, and guess what, nothing changed. It lasted a couple of months, and as quickly as the calls started, they soon ended. No reason, no explanation, no lie. Just no more calls.

I believe the calls stopped coming because he realized I was no longer a pushover. I challenged him more than I ever had. I opened up and told him how I felt every time he left me. I told him everything. I was still hurt and emotionally drained by the so-called relationship we had in the past. I needed to release all those emotions. I needed those old wounds to heal. As we talked, I challenged him to be truthful with me and himself. I asked him to take a good, long look at his life and tell me why he was still alone. I wanted him to think about his life and how he has passed up real happiness for a mirage. Don't get me wrong, his real happiness wasn't centered around me. Real happiness must be centered around God. Real happiness comes with knowing Jesus. With all the talks we had, he never once said he was happy. He spoke about many regrets and some moments that brought him joy, but somehow, that happiness that he desired had never been accomplished as of that moment.

Many times, we can't seem to shake off our past because our emotions are still tied to them. Those ties can stunt our growth. They restrict us from being the person we want to be. I know for myself I can't live in the past. So I made a choice to let the past be just that—the past. All hurts, heartbreaks, foolish decisions are behind me. I look forward to the sunrise over the horizon of my future. A new day is dawning.

I survived on broken pieces.

Chapter 17

I Didn't Fit In

Many times, I found myself all alone and lonely because I didn't seem to fit in. I was never really part of a crew, click, or group. My body was present but I always felt out of place. I always felt that there had to be something better, something more fulfilling for me. Yes, I hung out with friends, family, or classmates in clubs, parties, and gatherings. The feeling was never right. I felt out of place all the time, but I went along to be a part of something because being alone, I was definitely part of nothing.

I went through the motions. I would drink because it helped me become another person. It numbed me to my true feelings.

Sure, there were times when I asked myself, *Why do I keep doing this? I don't like it but it is better than being alone.*

I'm from a large family, but I never really seemed to fit in there either. I felt out of place, even displaced at times. Those feelings of inadequacy followed me into my adult life.

When I was young, I accepted Jesus into my life as my Lord and Savior without really understanding what all that entailed. As I got older, I realized that my lifestyle was a little conservative for me. I wanted to experience things, so I backslid. I decided to go against my spiritual teaching. Bad move! It was then when I truly realized there was no place for me back in the old lifestyle.

I went back to clubs, partying day and night, but I could not enjoy myself not even after having a few drinks. It just wasn't the same. I was extremely uncomfortable, although I tried hard not to show it. I was that dog that turned to his own vomit.

It's amazing that I thought I could fit in a place that I didn't fit into at first. That's what Satan does. He has us confused to the point where we don't remember how bad something was until we found ourselves back in it again.

When I would drink, it didn't taste right. When I tried to hang out with a group, play cards, dominos, talk trash, and cuss, I felt so out of place. I enjoyed dancing, but I couldn't seem to get into the groove. And I could not understand why.

It wasn't until many years later while sitting in the beauty shop. I heard a sermon entitled God is married to the back slider. I listened because that was me. The word of God will find you. I was in a back-slider state. I left Jesus in search of better things, or so I thought. As I listened to the sermon, I said to myself, *Jesus is married to me? How could that be?*

I gave up on him in search for a more glamorous lifestyle. That was definitely an illusion. I began to think on those words. Jesus is married to me, and he is trying to get my attention in subtle ways. He is letting me know that he still loves me. I thought, *God still loves me? I pushed him aside, walked out on him for what appeared to be something better, I turned my back on him, and he still loves me. How is that possible?* I began to think, *God had once delivered me from a life of sin, and he didn't want me to go back into it.* Like many before me, I thought the grass was greener on the other side. I thought life was better as a sinner. It was like I wanted a divorce and God wanted to stay married. So he kept chasing after me in subtle ways, watching over me, wanting me to come back to him. At first, I didn't understand. But in his own sweet, gentle, and sometimes stern way, He was telling me, "I have married you. I have shown you a better life. You don't belong to that old lifestyle anymore. I forgave you of those old ways. I have given you a new life when you accepted me. I changed you, I washed you clean, and I saved you from yourself."

"Come back to me." Those sweet words seemed to echo in my heart. It was as if I could feel his very presence. I began to ponder even more why I didn't fit in anymore with certain people, with that worldly lifestyle. It was because God did not intend for me to live life outside of him. He didn't intend for me to be a part of that crew. He has a different plan for me and for you.

I know now what the Lord God has for us. It's a love that can't be explained, a love the human mind cannot conceive. The kind of love that we are constantly looking for in others, from others, but they don't have that kind of love to give. Only God can offer pure love, unconditional love. He loves us in spite of whoever, whatever we may be.

God loves us so much that he sent his only son Jesus to die—not to live but die!

It's hard to let go of that kind of love. So if you are a backslider or you just find yourself not being able to fit in, just remember that where you are right now is not where you have to stay. Get it right and come home, home to God. I did; he is waiting on you! I'm grateful I survived on broken pieces.

Chapter 18

Forgiveness

It seems ironic how one word can cause a change to come about in our lives. That one word is *forgive*. Many of us hold on to past hurt for far too long. We keep playing the tune "Another Somebody Done Somebody Wrong" song over and over in our head.

We keep looking for someone to blame for our failures, regrets, lack of achievements, the reasons for not fitting in a particular circle of people, as well as our lack of motivation. Yes, someone may have been a contributing factor in your pain.

The fact remains you cannot and should not allow a person, or being in a bad situation take control of your life. When you walk around day in and day out with unforgivingness in your heart, you have given someone control over your life.

We may feel our reasons are legitimate, but why have we allowed another person that much control over us? If we give others control, this means we are allowing them to manipulate our life. They are pulling our strings. They have become the puppet master, and we're the one who moves at their command. The puppet master has total control and authority over you, the puppet.

There was an incident that occurred in my life. I was in my mid-twenties. It involved only a couple of family members at first as this incident began to escalate. It started to involve more and more of my family, siblings, nieces, cousins this is how I know all too well how people can be controlled by others and why there is such a need to forgive.

As I looked back at the situation, this one person controlled me and in fact controlled a great number of my family members. This was a life-altering experience for me. For me, there was nothing more devastating than the hurt of being rejected by family. To be an outcast because some people were trying to make themselves look good. The whole situation solely existed as a cover-up for something they had done, and they thought I was going to spill the beans. Of course they didn't know me at all because I would not have said anything. I don't thrive on others getting hurt.

This situation became extremely unbearable for me. I hurt for years. I cried for years. I ached and had a sick feeling in the pit of my stomach for years. I seemingly wanted to just vomit. This was the thing that almost took me out. I was an emotional wreck. This person controlled me. She started by telling lies on me and then things got worse. She talked about me, degraded me to my family, mutual friends, and to my belief, anyone who would listen. This made it unbearable for me to face anyone because they all believed her. I could never be comfortable around anyone I knew she talked to and especially not my family because they believe her lies.

She loved to talk, and she had a personality that would draw people to her. She was always the life of the party. We all know this type of person who always has to be the center of attention no matter what.

My family was always doing something. There was always a gathering. There were no mistakes about how she felt about me, and eventually, I began to resent her. In order to further attempt to keep me away from the family, she would make sure she planned events at her house, ensuring I wouldn't come because I knew I was not welcome.

This was a situation out of control. I already had self-esteem issues due to past events in my life, so I can only think I was an easy target. I became very withdrawn during that time, and this went on for years. One thing after another with this person who is my sister-in-law. So now do you see how personal it was? I will not go into any more detail right now. I just wanted you to get the picture and understand the role of control and the need for forgiveness. There were many things that hurt me down through the years, but being estranged from people I truly loved was the worst.

I have a cousin who was like a sister to me. She got to her too. I am sharing this because I allowed someone to control me to the point that when my cousin was hanging on for her life, I did not go to the hospital to see her. Why? Because of fear of intimidation. I couldn't bear the thoughts of being alone with the family who were strangers to me. They were clueless as to who I was. I could imagine the stares and the whispers. I had been through that before when one of our aunts was in the hospital. I wasn't strong enough emotionally to endure that again. I convinced myself that I just couldn't go to see her. I felt terrible. I didn't go, but every time I made up my mind to go, fear and anxiety would grip me as if someone wrapped me like a mummy. Not going cost me to lose the closeness I had with my cousin. We don't have that same bond anymore. I asked her to forgive me and she did, but it was so hard for me to forgive myself. I let her down. I let someone I love down. Now she shares that closeness with my younger sister. I'm okay with that, but I know firsthand what allowing someone to have control over you can cost.

When things of this magnitude happens in your life, you can't help but to be hurt, angry, bitter, and resentful. That's why forgiveness is so important. If you don't forgive, those emotions will spill over into other areas of your life and affect your actions and reactions toward others.

As time passed, many tears and much prayer to God allowed some of my family to see sides of her that at one time only I could see. Please understand that I am not bashing my sister-in-law. I love her, and I never thought I would be able to sincerely let those words come out of my mouth. But when God puts His love in you, everything changes.

Gradually, restoration came to me and my family through the grace and mercy of the true and living God.

I want people to understand the depth of control. Not only was I controlled by being kept away from my family, but my family was also controlled because they believed her so nobody reached out to me. Nobody wanted to hear what I had to say. Ironic, huh? They should have reached out. We were family. We played together, slept in the same bed, walked the same paths, yet we allowed one person to come between us for years, to make us forget we are family. And nothing should have broken that bond. Life happens, and we find sometimes that even in the best of families, a disruption can occur.

I had to let it all go. It was eating me until I was literally sick. Not a day went by that I didn't think of the wrong that was done to me. This would have taken me out had it not been for God.

Now I can smile again, walk with my head up again. I have renewed confidence, and it started with forgiveness. I released all that old stuff that had me sinking as if I were in quicksand. I was drowning until God threw me a lifeline.

I was introduced to Jesus early in my life, and I was able to recall some of the things I read in his word. This scripture came to me as I was telling God how much I loved him and was so grateful to him. Mark 11:24–25 (KJV) says, "And when ye stand praying forgive if ye have aught against any; that your father also which is in heaven my forgive you your trespasses. But if you do not forgive, neither will your father which is in heaven forgive your trespasses." It is clear that I have to forgive man or woman in order for God to forgive me.

I believe in God. Better yet, I believe God as I allowed that to sink in, and yes, it was a process. I knew I wanted to allow God's thoughts to marinate in my heart and mind. I know I wanted better. I wanted to feel better about myself, but most of all, I wanted to be free from the pain. The mental anguish was going to kill me, and I knew that if I died with unforgivingness in my heart, I was going straight to a burning hell to be tormented for eternity.

You can say what you will, but hell is real and I don't want to go there. My thought was, *I'm living my hell here. Why die and suffer even more than I can imagine?*

I realized Jesus is my advocate, my savior. All I had to do was ask him to forgive me, and he would and did. The next step was to forgive myself, which was almost as difficult as forgiving other people mainly because of the reminders, the thoughts that continue to go through my head. There is another entity at work trying to keep me in bondage. That enemy is Satan, the devil, an evil spirit or whatever you choose to call him. He is, in fact, real and will do anything to keep you in bondage.

As much as I hate being alone, so does Satan. He wants you in hell with him to be tormented for eternity. So let's weigh the options: forgive and have peace, or not forgive and continue to be constantly tormented. For me, the choice is peace. I knew I had endured this type of punishment long enough.

One thing we fail to understand is when we allow others to control our lives. We sometimes get hurt or angry, and anger can soon turn to bitterness, then hate settles in your heart like you settle into your favorite chair.

Now let's face it. Once you've established a comfortable position, you don't want to move. That's how Satan is. He has decided to permanently fix himself to you by making you believe you are justified by the way you feel, and we being humans, that somehow makes us feel good but only for a short time.

On the other hand, there is a still, quiet voice telling you something is wrong. Then comes a battle in your mind: good versus evil; what's right and what's wrong. Hurting people definitely hurt other people; that's a fact. It is learned behavior. Everyone wants to guard their heart, and rightly so.

No one wants to endure pain. My best advice to you is to do what I did: listen to that quiet voice, hear those sweet whispers telling you to forgive. Forgive those who used you, hurt you, and abused you. It won't be easy, but God will be with you every step of the way throughout the entire process. He won't leave you. He can truly take the pain away. Once you have forgiven others, forgive yourself. It's okay.

There is a purpose for your going through what you've been through. You may not believe it, you may not be able to see it, but as time goes on, you will. Behind the scene, God is working. Just let go. Let the process take place. Before you know it, your heart will be filled with joy, love, peace, and happiness.

Forgiveness has brought all of that into my life and more. The only one I want to have control over my life is the one and only true and living God. I submit myself to him. I choose to live for him because he and only he has made my life a living testimony. I don't hold my head down anymore. I'm not sad, angry, or depressed anymore. I don't blame myself or others anymore. I have life. I am full of growth and potential. I have purpose. John 10:10 (NKJV) says, "The thief cometh not, but for to steal, and to kill and to destroy. I am come that the might have life and that they might have it more abundantly." Jesus said, "I came to give you life." I, for one, don't want his life or death to be in vain.

Forgiveness puts the ball back in your court. It gives control back to you, and who better control your life than the living God and you!

I survived on broken pieces

Chapter 19

Learning to Love Yourself

Where do I start? How do I begin to love myself? These are the questions I ask myself. I discovered that first of all, I have to know myself. I have to shed all the faces and cover-ups and get down to the basics, the bare element of my soul.

My soul, my deepest, innermost being. The person I was created to be. I had to shed that person who wasn't me, like snakes shed their skin. I had packed on layers upon layers of clothing, such as other people's thoughts and opinions of me. I was weighted down so heavily that I felt hunched over, barely able to put one foot in front of the other.

The time came when I had to let it all go: shed the dead weight, strip away the layers of having no joy, no happiness, and low self-esteem. My mind had to be totally stripped of the thoughts and opinions of others. Only then would I be able to stand up straight. I had to be willing to shed all the relationships that went wrong, the things that were said and done in those relationships that ended with me being gossiped about and hurt, the things that left me feeling lower than low, the one I thought should have loved me but didn't. I had to shed the feeling of worthlessness, inadequacy, depression, anger, bitterness, not measuring up to the expectation of others, and the need to be validated by others. The list goes on.

Take off the former things, the stuff that's weighing you down, and be willing to take on the new. Don't be afraid to see yourself for who you are, without the makeup. You may feel apprehension as you stand naked looking at yourself for who you truthfully are without the preconceived notions of others. Take a good look at who you are.

Now the word of God in Psalms 139:14 says that we are wonderfully made. So, really, whose opinion counts over God's? I had to believe this, and I was willing to say what God said about me. As you stand in the mirror of your mind, smile. You may not know where this is leading you, but understand that it is the beginning of something new.

Once you have shed those layers for the new you, it's time to learn to love yourself. You will realize that you too have survived on broken pieces.

I had been looking for others to define me, to love me. And now standing naked, I know I must define myself, love myself. I have to start with forgiving myself for all the mistakes, stupid decisions, the character flaws, the masquerade, and the actor I played in other people's movies. We know in many instances we only acted the part to get or try to get someone's approval.

Forgive yourself for losing yourself. When we take on a character from someone else's screenplay, we have a tendency to lose ourselves and take on the role of the person we are playing, the actor. And even after the movie is completed, we still continue to act the part. Acting causes us to lose our true identity and become someone else.

That's what many of us have done, and that's why we can't love ourselves. We have applied the characteristics and identity of someone other than our self, and now that the play is over, we don't know who we are. And we can't love that which we do not know.

There is one person who knows us and can help us get to know ourselves. He is God the Father and the creator of all things. He knows you, he formed you, he knew you before you we formed in your mother's womb. God has a plan for our lives. He wants to prosper us. He tells us in his word in Isaiah 43:18–19, "Remember ye not the former things, neither consider the things of old behold I do a new things."

You may ask, how do I get to the Father in order to understand these things he promised? You get to the Father by the way of his son Jesus Christ. Ask the Father for forgiveness of your wrongdoings, failures, and sins. Believe that Jesus lived, died, and rose from the dead. Once you have asked God to forgive you, forgive yourself then take on the characteristics of your Heavenly Father and Jesus his son.

"Therefore if any man be in Christ He is a new creature, old things are passed away, behold all things are become new" (2 Cor. 5:17, KJV).

Get to know him. Lose yourself in Christ Jesus, and in return, you will find yourself.

I survived on broken pieces

Chapter 20

The Process

When we give our life to Christ, there is no magic wand that is going to erase all the wrong we've done or the wrong that had been done to us, but accepting Christ will help you face it and forgive yourself and others.

The word of God does tell us we will reap what we sow. That doesn't change just because you have accepted Christ. What does happen is that God will be there with you as you go through the process of reaping.

We used to say of a person that they can dish it out but they can't take it. When you say words to someone that cause emotional harm, or physical pain or carry malice in your heart toward someone, God knows and you will reap what you've sown in some form or fashion. We have to understand that Gods word is Gods word and he will not change it for anyone.

You must take the first step, which is usually the hardest. There is a debate going on in your mind to accept Christ or not. You have to choose. No one can make the decision for you; it is an individual choice.

Once you have accepted Christ, ask him for the gift of the Holy Spirit, who will lead you and guide you into all truth. When we accept Christ, we must walk in the truth of his word. In order for this to happen, we must read the word of God. His word is alive. His words are powerful, his word is strength to you. The more you read his words, God will give you understanding. All you have to do is ask.

This is all a process. It all takes time. Don't get frustrated because change isn't coming as quickly as you hoped.

Faith has to be developed. We have to continually hear the word and read the word in order for our faith to be strengthened. Our belief in God and our trust in God are all by faith. This walk that we have chosen is a faith walk. We must believe that God is there and he is watching over us as well as taking care of us.

The word tells us that without faith, it is impossible to please God. We must believe that God is God and we must diligently seek him. We must look for him continually. God wants us to trust, believe and obey him and only him. With God all things are possible to them that believe.

Yes, you will cry. But know God loves you enough to bottle your tears, and his words will comfort you.

Yes, you will experience loss, but God says I'll never leave you. Yes, people will still talk about you, lie about you, but God will be your vindicator. The word lets us know that vengeance belongs to God and he will repay. All you need to do is pray. Tell God what hurts you, what concerns you. He will fix it all in time. God does everything in time, and that is in his time, not ours. It is all a process; we didn't just get where we are in a blink of the eye. It was a process. Growth in Christ is a process too. Enjoy the ride knowing that the Greater One is in you, and nothing happens to you that God doesn't know first.

God loves his children, and that's who we are when we accepted Jesus Christ as our Lord and Savior. We become a child of God. As a child of God, you become righteous, you become Holy, you become redeemed from your past. The past has no more authority over you. God will crown us with righteousness, and He will not withhold anything from us as long as we walk holy and righteous before him with a pure heart.

We cannot hold iniquity in our hearts. Our hearts must be clean. We have to do as David in Psalms 51. Cry out to God to create in you a clean heart. God has to create a clean heart in us. We were born to sin. So God has to change our heart and he has to renew a right spirit in us. One reason we come to God is that our spirit is broken and we need to be restored from the old to the new. We need heart surgery. We need to be fixed by our maker, our creator, the one who knows all about us.

God knows our thoughts before we think them, our words before we speak them, and our actions before we expose them. God knows everything. He knows if our repentance is sincere or just a means to try to escape something. God knows us. So don't think you can fool God; you can't. Come to God with sincerity of heart and he will make all things new. In 2 Corinthians 5:17, it says that if any man be in Christ, he is a new creature. Old things no longer exist. You are free from them. All things are to become new. Accept the new, a new life in Christ Jesus.

I survived on broken pieces

Chapter 21

When You Love So Much, You Have to Release It

We start with that age-old question: What is love? Love means different things to different people. Love is an extremely strong emotion. It is the tie that binds people together long after everything else has been torn apart.

Love is strong enough to keep that abused wife from leaving her husband. Love keeps that mother holding on to that drug-addicted child who's stealing from her. Love keeps us holding on to that rebellious child. Love is the thing that keeps us holding on when in our hearts we know it's time to let go. Love keeps us holding on to those who have shown us that they don't want us, but we are determined not to let go. Love is a powerful emotion. Some of us would rather go without food than love. Some of us turn to food because of love, especially if that love is not reciprocated. Love keeps us holding on even when every fiber in us tells us we need to let it go.

I know it's not easy, but in the long run, you will see as I did. It all worked out for my own good.

I held on to a relationship that was unhealthy for me for far too long. This man had me mesmerized. I was so captivated by his charm that I could not shake him. I love so much about him, but he was poison to me. It took many years, and I finally figured it out. I was ashamed and embarrassed. It took me so long, but I was bound to his charm. His smile just made my heart melt. Although he was a good liar and he battled with drugs, I still hoped for the man he once was, the man I fell in love with. That man never returned. I had to face the harsh reality that if I didn't let him go, all my dreams would vanish. I spent too much time and energy holding on to someone who was not holding on to me.

There are times in our lives when we tend to love too much. We still try to hold on to the very thing that God wants us to let go of. We have to be liberated, set free from situations and circumstances in our life. It doesn't matter if it's an intimate relationship, a child, or even a family member, sometimes we just have to let it go! God doesn't want us to forsake the situation altogether. We don't just kick them to the curb; we continue to love. But don't be fooled any longer.

God's desire is that we give it to him and let him work it out. The situation or circumstance has disrupted our peace and taken our thoughts entirely off God, who he is, and what he can do.

God is a jealous God. He doesn't want us to love anyone or anything more than we love him. That's why a lot of relationships do not work out. Because think about it, who are you putting first in your life? The word of God in Matthew 22:37–38 says, "Love the Lord with all thy heart, with all thy soul and with all thy mind. This is the first and great commandment." Some of you may not have accepted Jesus as Lord and Savior yet, but know those words are for believers and nonbelievers alike. God comes first, and he will allow all others things to fall in place.

You may not realize it, but that husband, child, family member, job, home, and money can be distractions that can creep in and take the place of God because we love so deeply and so strongly.

There are times when we must step aside and release the situation to God. You are holding on to something you have no control over. You can't change it. It is not in your power to do so. If you could, you would have changed it already. God is in charge.

I love my family greatly. I was willing to jump through hoops for them. I began to ask God why I loved them so much, why my burden for them seemed so heavy. God revealed to me that I was making them my God. I was more concerned about how they perceived me than how God saw me. I was so wrapped up in wanting them to love me that I forgot about God himself who gave me life. I was allowing the love I had for them to cloud my vision of the realness of God's love toward me. Everything that I wanted and needed, or so I thought, was wrapped up in their acceptance of me. The situation as a whole had consumed me. All I could think about was wanting their love and validation.

One day, God took me on a journey and allowed me to see that I was holding on, hanging on for their approval of me, something that I didn't need because I have been accepted by my beloved Savior Jesus Christ.

Through that journey through the mirror of life, God revealed I need him more than anything. It doesn't matter how you try to hold on to that love; you need to realize that it's time to release it. Give it to God. He is the one who can handle it. He has shoulders broad enough to take on your burdens. Once you have truly turned it loose, God will be able to restore it back to you if that is his will. We must be careful and understand that God's will and our will are different. We must ask God to conform our will with his will.

So I'm saying to you, when you find yourself loving so much that it hurts, you can't function. When love consumes your very being, release it; let it go! Allow God to restore what is needed in you. Take away what has a tendency to hold you back. Pour yourself into God and he will in turn pour himself into you. Draw near to God and he will draw near to you. Accept God's perfect will for your life, then and only then will things be far better for you than you can imagine. God is just awesome like that. He is how I survived on broken pieces.

Chapter 22

Judgmental

We sometimes tend to be judgmental of others because there is something lacking in our own lives. Being judgmental of others seems to lessen our own insecurities. If we can point out the flaws of others, somehow that diminishes their worth in the eyes of others, and for a moment, you are able to forget about your own insecurities.

Some of us are so busy trying to make sure that a tiny, insignificant thing in someone else's life is magnified so that no one will see the brokenness in ours.

Brokenness often causes us to become quick to judge, criticize, and point out the character flaws of others. Oftentimes, it's not always what we see. Oftentimes it's what we hear or have heard that causes us to become judgmental.

We are people who make our assumptions of people by the words of others. Who is to say that what is being said to us is truth?

This is one truth I do know. The words of God says in Matthew 7:1–2 (NLT), "Do not judge others and you will not be judged. For you will be treated as you treat others. The standard you use in judging is the standard by which you will be judged." Think about those words the next time you want to belittle or criticize someone.

We don't like having to face who we are, but until we are able to face ourselves—our true selves—only then will we be able to move on to another phase in our life. I realize this may be a hard pill to swallow; it was for me.

So many times I found something wrong with everybody and everything around me. I was out of control; I mean, I was critical of the simplest things such as someone's clothing, hair, teeth, weight, anything to take the focus off me and my own issues. I was quick to judge others because I often didn't like what I saw in the mirror. I was hanging on by a thread. I was messed up from being judged so much of my life I thrived on being critical and judgmental toward others. I finally realized why I was so quick to be hard on others; it was due to my own sense of insecurity.

I eventually had to face the harsh reality that the treatment I received was the same treatment I had at some point in my life given out. I knew if I didn't change my words, my conversation, I would continue the same cycle— by speaking negatively of others I could only receive negative in return. That's the law of sowing and reaping. Send negativity out, receive negativity back. Proverbs 6:2 (KJV) says you are snared by the words of your mouth. Now I understand that to mean You have just set your own trap for yourself by your words." I had entangled myself with the words from my mouth when I belittled and criticized others.

But I found out that the words of God are awesome. It will always give you a way out if you want it, and I wanted it. I was so sick of being negative that at times, I couldn't stand myself. I'm sure those who were around me were sick of me as well. They just didn't say it.

These two scriptures have been helpful to me to keep my focus: Proverbs 18:21 (NJKV), "Death and life are in power of the tongue." The words that you speak can be positive and bring life and growth, or negative and bring destruction and death. Your words can be used to build up or to tear down. How do you choose to use the words that come out of your mouth? Matthew 12:36–37 (NLT) you will give account on judgment day for every idle word you speak. Our words will either acquit us or condemn us. In simple term, the right words will save your life; the wrong words spoken out of your mouth will condemn you to hell, and that is no laughing matter.

There is power in the words we speak. Use those words for good and not evil, to build up and not tear down. It's your life, your future. But for me, I have chosen to speak positively, and positivity flows in my life today.

I survived on broken pieces.

Chapter 23

The Road to Here
A Highway of Life

Where is here? Here is my place of peace, my place of rest, my place of comfort. A place of faith, my wealthy place. No, not monetary wealth, but a wealth of peace, better understanding, wisdom, confidence, love, and security with myself.

The road to here was full of bumps, potholes, and pit stops. There were times when my engine stalled, my temperature gauge ran hot, and my tires blew.

There were stoplights I ran through that caused me to crash and burn. The accidents left me shaken, bruised, and sometimes broken. But still, somehow I survived as I continued on the road to here.

As I continued on this road, I picked up some people and some of their things along the way—some good, some not so good—as I went from destination to destination. I picked up Mr. Pride, Mr. Stubborn, Ms. Liar, Ms. Unforgivingness, Ms. Bitterness, Mr. Broke, Mr. I-Can't-Find-a-Job, Mr. Lazy, Ms. Lack-of-Confidence, Ms. Arrogant, and Mr. I-Don't-Need-You-to-Make-Me-Look-Good as I traveled down the road to here.

There were times when I fell asleep at the wheel only to awaken before falling over a cliff. I took detours and ended up in places I had no business in. I ran through caution lights without looking to make sure the road way was clear. I failed to take the time to ease around sharp curves before shifting into high gears, not giving thought to safety.

I picked up hitchhikers alone the way. They had no clue where they wanted to go nor how to get there. But after a while, I realized they just wanted to ride. They never wanted to drive—always following, never leading. When they see you're tired, weary, and sleep deprived, they will still not take control of the wheel. Eventually, you find yourself pulling over for gas. While they are using the restroom or buying some snacks, you drive off continuing on the road to here.

Many people including myself have traveled this road. Some of you may have taken the detour and you haven't arrived yet, but rest assured you will get here if you don't run out of gas. You have to continue to fuel up. If you don't, you will find yourself stranded in the middle of nowhere.

So now, the trip you thought would take a few days turned into a few years traveling down the road to here.

As you traveled, you picked up some precious cargo along the way by the name of faith, and hope. They became the reason why you would get your oil change, have a tune-up, and the tires rotated. Faith and hope reminded you to stop at the stop sign. To go slowly through the caution light and pull over once in a while to smell the roses, admire the clouds, and just sit and feel the warmth of the sun on your face.

The thing about the road to here is that we are so hurried to get somewhere. So many of us don't map out our course, and although they may use a GPS and take turn-by-turn instructions, we may still end up having to take a detour while traveling down the highway of life. There are times when we know where we're headed, but we still get sidetracked. And before we knew it, we have passed our exit. Some of us may be able to back up, get on the right exit, and continue on. Some of us have to keep going a few miles before we can get back on the right road. Yet others just turn around. Again, this is where that precious cargo—faith and hope—comes into play. They will tell us, "Don't turn around. Keep straight. You'll soon find the right road." As you continue to travel, you think about all the bumps, potholes, pit stops, detours, and hitchhikers you ran into along the way. You say to yourself, *If it had not been for the many distractions, I would have been much farther up the road.*

As you continue to travel, you make stops to fuel up. Faith and hope are starting to grow on you. You soon pick up courage, a little joy, and some laughter, and soon, contentment settles in. Finally, you pick up peace. One day, you pull on the side of the road, with the sunlight on your face, you look over at faith and hope and you smile. And at that very moment, you take a deep breath, hold it, and exhale. It is then that you'll realize you are here! You have arrived. You made it through the bad relationships, the low self-esteem, the abuse, the trials, the snares, and shortcomings. The things that should have made you sit idle, you made it through.

I have come into my wealthy place of peace, contentment, and faith in God to believe that if I continue on the road to here, from here I will make it there.

Where is there? It is much more of what I have found on the road to here: more love, joy, peace, happiness, temperance, meekness, the fruits of the spirit found in Galatians 5:22-23 (KJV).

Enjoy the ride if God is in you and you're in him. You will end up just where you should be: traveling down the highway of life.

Always remember the rearview mirror is made to glance back. We need to stop looking back at what we've been through and look forward to what we are going into. Paul said it best in Philippians 3:13 (KJV): "Brethren I count not myself to have apprehended but this one thing I do forgetting those things which are behind and reaching forth unto those things which are before."

Stop looking back. Stop regretting what didn't happen or what did. Embrace where God is taking you.

I survived on broken pieces

Chapter 24

My Agreement

When I started out, so much of this was hurtful to write about. I struggled within myself about putting so much of me in these pages for all to see. I thought, *What will people think of me? Will they think as others did in my life that I'm crazy, stupid, or no way would I open up like that.* Then God reminded me of what I told him after he delivered me. I said I would share my life as an open book, a testimony for his glory. Without him by my side, I would never have made it. I was broken, shattered, and had no one to pick up the pieces but God!

God saw something in me that I didn't see—couldn't see—in myself. All of this is for his glory, and my prayer is that something in the pages of this book will find you and that you will find Jesus and let him be your Lord and Savior. It's because of the love that Jesus has for me that I am alive. If it had been left up to the forces that were working against me, I would have been long gone a distant memory. God saw greatness in me and he see greatness in you. In fact greatness is in all of us who choose Christ. First John 4:4 (KJV) says, "Greater is he that is in you than he that is in the world." Greater means I'm good enough. Greater means I can handle whatever comes upon me. Christ is greater than any adversity.

The truth remains that no matter how low you feel, how marred you are by life, what pit you may find yourself in, know that God will deliver you even if it's from yourself. If you find that you are your own worst enemy due to the thoughts you think and the avenue you have chosen to walk down, know that you are not beyond God's ability to repair.

There were many times in my life when I've felt lower than a snake's belly because of poor choices and situations I found myself in. but God never left me; he was there. He doesn't want us to make bad choices, but we do. It's in our DNA. We were born in sin. Our nature is to do just that and we will. That's why forgiveness from God is available to all who choose him. When we give our lives to God, that's when a transformation takes place. In 2 Corinthians 5:17 (NKJV), it says, "Therefore if anyone is in Christ, he is a new creature; old things have passed away, behold all things have become new."

I thought about the caterpillar that crawls, only seeing what's in front of it. But one day, there is a transformation and the ugly thing that once crawled has become a beautiful creation that flies and is admired for its beauty. As God transformed a creature into a creation, allow him to change you. Nothing is impossible for God.

I believe, and God has made and is still making the impossible possible, not just for me but for many wonderful people who are a part of my life. God truly has given me beauty for ashes! I love him. It's because of God that I survived on broken pieces.

Chapter 25

The Cost Jesus Paid It All

We suffer needlessly in so many situations in our life. We fight against others and we fight against ourselves. So many things we war against are unnecessary. Many of the battles in our mind and the losses we suffer can be avoided if only we would give our lives to Christ.

Jesus loves us; he paid the ultimate price. He gave his life for us. I wonder sometimes if we really thought about what Jesus went through so that we could have a better life on this earth as well as in heaven.

Imagine yourself being on this earth and knowing that you must die for the sins of the world although you have not committed one single sin. Can you imagine what it is like to anticipate death, knowing that no matter what you do, it is still coming?

Jesus was in human form, in flesh and blood. He experienced hurt, pain, fatigue, love, dishonor, and humiliation just as we sometimes do.

Everybody Jesus met was not good to him. They didn't recognize him as savior of the world, just as people don't recognize your worth at times. Jesus was just the son of Mary and Joseph, brother to James and John.

Although they saw the miracles, many still did not believe that he is the Messiah. During Jesus's lifetime, many people were full of unbelief, just as it is now. People don't believe who Jesus is. Jesus a man that walked this earth, who was filled with love and compassion, his mission was to save the loss, to save us from ourselves. We were sinners with no hope. Jesus came and gave us hope at the cost of his own life. Jesus felt the pain of his approaching death. He began to worry because he knew the agony that he would soon face. He went to the garden to pray to God our Father to let this cup pass. He prayed, "I don't want to do this, I don't want to endure this pain." The thought of the cross was too much for Jesus at that moment, his prayer so intense that sweat fell from his face like great drops of blood. I can imagine sweat falling from Jesus's face and the tears of anguish he must have shed as he prayed so earnestly. As Jesus prayed as he talked to the Father and the Father talked back to him, I can see Jesus began to be assured to rest in the words of his Father so comfortably that he responded, "Nevertheless not my will by thine be done." Jesus humbly submitted his will to God the Father's will, to suffer pain like no other for us.

I wonder if we have really thought about what Jesus suffered and to what extreme he suffered. Go on this journey with me and understand that Jesus body is just like ours. As an innocent man, he was taken captive and led from one court of law to another because people wanted him to be found guilty. They wanted to find a judge who would pronounce the guilty sentence on him although the only thing he was guilty of was love and compassion. It's shameful that the world we live in will punish you for caring.

The mistreatment Jesus suffered was like none other. He was beaten, battered, and bruised. He was spit on, mocked, and even had a crown of thorns pressed onto his head. Jesus was beaten to the point that he was unrecognizable even to his family.

Can you imagine the hurt his mother, Mary, felt? The bitter anguish she went through as her son was beaten, as the very flesh was pulled off his body with each crack of a whip? And yet Jesus never said a word. He endured all of this for us. Many of us can't stand to be talked about without wanting to lash out. But Jesus kept quiet, no doubt all the time praying to the Father to give him the strength he needed to continue on to the cross. I want you to understand that Jesus's flesh was ripped open, bleeding. No doubt, wounds festering, and was in excruciating pain but still focused on us, still focused on his purpose of saving and redeeming souls back to the Father.

Jesus's body was hurting, stiff, sore, wounds still open, and was forced to carry a heavy piece of wood on his battered, painful, wounded back.

For a moment, as I imagine the hardship he endured as he carried the cross on those open wounds, I feel as if I can hardly breathe. The pain had to be as none I can even imagine.

Then I came to the realization of the fact that someone loved me that much. It brings me to tears, even sobs, to know I am loved. When I felt like my world was torn apart, when I wanted to end it all, when the depression was so dark there was not even a flicker of light, somehow I felt the love of Jesus. I remembered that he gave his life for me. Someone died for me so that I could have a better life!

Jesus endured the pain of being nailed with huge nails to a wooden cross. Nails in his hands, nails in his feet, being mocked, teased, and given vinegar to drink, Jesus was truly ostracized for no reason. He went about the region doing good. He knew they hated him. He knew he was going to die. But it didn't stop him from giving people hope, hope for a better life a life free of sin, shame from all the stigma that this world put on us. Jesus died so that we can be free! Now understand that the death of the cross wasn't the end for Jesus. He has risen. He came out of the grave, and he is in heaven making intercession for us. He is our mediator, our advocate. You see, Jesus was one of us. He felt the woes of society. He felt the heartache of mankind. He knows what it's like to love and that love not be returned.

We break apart into pieces when we feel people don't love us like we think they should. Do you ever think how Jesus feels? He loves us so much that he gave his life, yet some of us treat him as if he's done nothing. We act as if he doesn't exist. We are to acknowledge Jesus, worship, and honor him. Praise him, thank him, adore him because he took the time to come from glory to earth. He loved his Father and us until he said, "I will be a living sacrifice for the sins of the world." Jesus endured it all for us. The cost was great, but Jesus paid it all. He gave his life, his all for us. Why can't we give our all for him? It's because of Jesus that I survived on broken pieces, and you can too!

Chapter 26

Transformed by the Word of God

For so long, I answered to whatever they called me, and because of that, I became my own worst enemy and my biggest critic.

As I began to read the word of God, I could see transformation take place in my life. Romans 12:2 (AMP) reads, "And do not be conformed to this world (any longer with its superficial values and customs) but be transformed and progressively change (as you mature spiritually) by the renewing of your mind. (focusing on Godly values and ethical attitudes) so that you may prove (for yourselves) what the will of God is, that which is good and acceptable and perfect (in his plan and for his purpose for you)."

The things of the world, the things that only matter on the surface, such as how I dress, what designer labels do I wear, how I wear my hair, what car I drive, these are thoughts and values of others. The things that matter on the surface where people can see, these mean nothing to God.

God is concerned about what your inner person looks like. God examines the heart. Everything else will turn to dust or rust.

When God begins his transformation process on you, he says in Isaiah 43:18 (AMP), "Do not remember the former things or ponder the things of the past." He goes on to say in verse 25, "I, only I am he who wipes out your transgression for my own sake. And I will not remember your sins." That's good news. Ponder on that for a moment. God will not remember your former identity, who or what you were called by, once you've asked him to forgive your sins.

"Listen carefully I am about to do a new thing now it will spring forth, as you began to read and meditate on his word new life and new beginning will spring forth." I've become a servant to God, not to man, not to Satan, and not to the superficial thing of this world, but to God and him alone. I owe my life to God, and I mean that my entire life has changed because of him and by him.

God is the very beat of my heart, the very air that fills my lungs. He is the reason that I'm still here. He is the reason for the smile on my face every blessed morning and through my day.

God is! There is no limit. He just is, whoever, whatever, however you need him to be. He is there. He is my provider, my peace, my joy, my helper, my strength, to name a few.

God has been called a wheel in the middle of a wheel. The rose of Sharon, Lily of the valley. I just call on him and he answers. He doesn't always answer immediately, but I wait. While I wait, I think on his words. His words renew and strengthen me. Isaiah 40:31 (AMP) says, "But those who wait for the Lord. (who expect, look for and hope in him) will gain strength and renew their power." This is part of the transformation. Isaiah goes on to say, "They will run and not become weary."

I run for God as hard and as fast as I ran for Satan. I have had days where I was tired in my body and my spirit; but when I began to think about all that God has brought me through, how he kept me from danger that I could see as well as danger that was not obvious to me. I became energized all over again.

Run for God. Don't get weary. Don't get tired of doing what is right, what is pleasing to God. In return, you will gain a great reward for your labor. God wants us to labor for him with our witness, our life, and the way we treat others.

Jesus told his disciples after he had fed the multitude, "Gather the fragments, gather that which remains that is usually lost, looked over, tossed aside, gather so that nothing be lost." Jesus wants us all to come to him with our broken pieces, fragmented hearts, or whatever pieces maybe left of us. We are still useful to God.

God made victorious people from fragments. Paul was a chief sinner who persecuted the church; he was fragmented. Rahab was a harlot; she was fragmented. Jeremiah was called the weeping prophet, fragmented. David had a man killed for his wife—fragmented. Moses stuttered and was fragmented.

We have many examples before us. So don't get weary; they didn't. They were on a mission, and so are we. Their outcome was historic; we still talk about them today.

Now that God has transformed us, will you leave your mark in history? Will your story be told? Will you share with others what God has done in your life? Will you be one who encourages, inspires, and gives a message of hope to those who will listen?

God has put greatness in all of us. Will you ask God to bring it out in you or will you hide the gifts and talents God has instilled in you so that God will not get the glory from your life? Be one who spreads the good news. Be one who will be bold and proclaim who Jesus is.

I am. I am redeemed, transformed, and renewed.

Thank God.

I survived on broken pieces.

Chapter 27

Inspiration

Surround yourself with people who inspire you, people who can help you transform your thinking and leave an impact on your life. That is what God allowed to happen to me.

God has paired me with wonderful people who have poured in my life. I am grateful.

I have learned how to be humbler by watching and being around one of humility. I've learned to revere God more by being around someone who has found Jesus for the first time. She has helped me remember the way I felt when I first accepted Jesus into my life. I've learned to be more joyous by watching someone blossom in the Lord. I see the love and joy in her eyes and I hear it in her voice. I've become more excited about this walk with God by being around one who has seen God change things in a matter of hours. I've watched someone change their words from "I can't because . . ." to "I can because of who God is." I have watched someone encourage others only to find out later they needed encouragement themselves. I have watched someone who's heart is so large that they just keep giving and giving expecting nothing in return.

These are the people I choose to celebrate because they have helped and encouraged me to be better, to be wiser, to be more compassionate. I challenge you, if you haven't found someone who encourages and inspires you to be better, find someone who encourages and inspires you through the word of God, as well as follows the will of God. I challenge you, if you are sincere about living for God, seek out people who inspire you and who will either plant seeds of greatness in you or water what is already planted.

If you are sincere about God, choose to obey his word. Choose to love in spite of what you may be going through. Love is not a choice; love is a commandment, basically an order. Like in the military, you are commanded to do certain things, and if you don't carry out that command, there are consequences. It's the same with God, but his consequences can be more severe. It can cost your soul, especially if you do not repent.

This year and in the coming years, I choose to walk with Jesus Christ. I choose to trust Him, believe him, and obey him, and no one or nothing will change that. If you choose to carry last year into this year, that's your choice. But don't expect me to come to that party. I'll pray for you that you allow God to change your heart, but I will not allow anyone to alter my destiny and neither should you.

Get inspired and get Jesus in your life.

Seek out those people who help build up and never tear down. Seek out those people who love God and who have heaven on their horizon. I promise you that if you do that, this year will be the start of a new life.

I choose to celebrate new life through Jesus Christ.

I survived on broken pieces.

Chapter 28

Feeling Weak Even When God Is There

I asked myself why, as women, we put ourselves through such emotional turmoil.

Why have we allowed others to make us feel less than God made us to be?

I'm reminded of Abram before he was Abraham when God told him to leave his country and get away from his kin.

There is no doubt Abram didn't want to go. He was comfortable. Everything around him was familiar. But God wanted him to be greater and have greater. No doubt God has put dreams and visions in us. But far too many of us fear man, fear failure, fear what others will think of us even those close to us. Some of us get ourselves in situations and we think God has no use for us, but I am a firm believer in the word of God. And he said in Jeremiah 29:11 (AMP), "I know the plans and thoughts that I have for you says The Lord plans for peace, and well being and not for disaster to give you a future and a hope."

God made a woman to be a helper to man. God made us to be wives, not live-in partners, not lovers, not mistresses, not friends with benefits. He said in Matthew 19:5 (KJV), "A man is to leave father and mother and shall cleave to his wife and they twain shall be one flesh."

God didn't make us to be abused and misused by our husbands, live-in partner, lover, or friends with benefits. So if God didn't make us for that purpose, why are we trying to remake ourselves?

In Psalms 139 (KJV), God said we are fearfully and wonderfully made. Meaning, he made us just like he wanted. God made us, so why should we allow a man to remake us, or why should we remake ourselves to fit someone's mold who's opinion is not greater than God's?

God made us in his likeness and image. He equipped us with what we need to survive.

Many of us settle into a way that is comfortable when we should be settling in the way that is God's.

Don't allow—and I say *allow* because you have to give up power, you have to give up control, you have to allow someone to restrain you.

Know that God Almighty equipped you with everything you need to survive, and survive you shall.

Remember that some of us are strong swimmers, some of us have life jackets, but the rest of us have to come in on broken pieces. Understand this: It doesn't matter how you get to God; just get to God! He is waiting for you. You will find peace and sweet, wonderful rest in God.

I survived on broken pieces.

Chapter 29

I Survived

The things between birth and death are called life. And in this life, we will have troubles.

We have to go through the loves we lost, the disobedient children we raised, the husband who's not attentive, the health that declines, the pit stops and potholes we are not expecting. All these are a part of life.

After reading this book some of you may ask why I retreated, why I didn't stand up for myself. The most likely answer is fear. Fear kept me in bondage. I was afraid that if I fought back, if I tried to defend myself, it would only make things worse. So I allowed things to happen. I've not been one who is confrontational or argumentative; to me, that settles nothing. In most cases, it only makes matters worse. I've always believed in God, and I believed somehow he would take care of me. And he did.

I had to go through everything that happened to me. It all had a part in my destiny. All of it was and is a part of God's perfect plan for my life. I didn't embrace it then, but I can embrace it now. I am a believer of the word of God, and his scripture in Isaiah 57:17 (NKJV) says, "No weapon formed against you shall prosper." I made it personal: no weapon formed against me shall prosper. The reason why I can say that is that I'm still here!

I am no longer bitter because of the things I went through, but I am better because I went through them.

I survived:

The childhood abuse I never talked to anyone about. That rape I never reported because it was a cousin.

That old man whom my family trusted who tried to fondle me.

Those boyfriends, or so I thought, who only used me.

Those girlfriends who only talked about, lied, and demeaned me.

Those so-called friends who only wanted to be around me for what they could get out of me.

Those family members who pushed me aside and acted like I was scum.

Those who said I'll never be anything.

Those who mentally, physically, and emotionally abused me.

The lover who was there for me only for his selfish gain.

The haters at my job who were always backstabbing me.

The church people who were gossiping about me. Most of them didn't even know me.

These crabs in a barrel who always tried to pull me down.

The family that thought I wasn't good enough to marry into their family.

To my childhood and high school best friends, or so I thought, who betrayed me.

To my brother whom I loved, but he discarded me out of his life like trash.

To my ex-husbands who never really understood me. (But it's okay.)

To all of you, I say thank you because if it were not for all of these, I would not be the woman I am today. I made it personal but it is not about me; it's for those who are hurting, those who need to forgive. God did it for me so he can do it for you. Know that you are not alone. I smile every day because I made it through those stormy seasons in my life.

Romans 8:28 (NKJV) says, "And we know that all things work together for good to those who love God, to those who are the called to his purpose." The scripture says "all things." I repeat, all things. I love God, and he loves me. Those things didn't feel good when I was in them. I had no clue that it would work out for my good. But I

know that now. For everything I went through, God was there. He never left me, and because of him and him only, I survived!
    No more broken pieces
    God has made me whole.

About the Author

S. Renee Brown was born and raised in a rural area of Arkansas. She is the tenth out of eleven children, with seven brothers and three sisters. She has resided in Pine Bluff, Arkansas, for the past twenty-three years. She is a licensed nurse who currently teaches at a local college. During her nursing career, she has provided care in the geriatric field. She enjoys caring for the elderly. Training others how to care for our seniors is an honor for her. She strongly believes that helping others is something that God has instilled in her.`

One of her daily prayers is that God will allow someone to cross her path to tell about his saving grace, his goodness, and how blessed we are, and to encourage them to live for Christ. She is very passionate, serious, and sensitive about the issues that affect women. Once broken and shattered herself, she heard the word of The Lord says come to me all ye that labor and are heavy laden, and I will give you rest. As she began to meditate on the word of God, he began to heal her broken, wounded spirit. God let her know that he put greatness in her. She began to write as her therapy to release the pain. She said God allowed her to see that she was not alone and He wanted her to share her story with others. Renee says it's not about where you've been or even about where you are right now, but where you're going that can impact your life the most. One of her missions in life is to encourage those who feel that life has dealt them an unfair hand. She is a firm believer in the words of Paul in Philippians 3:14: "I press toward the mark for the prize of the high calling of God in Christ Jesus." Run, continue to move forward no matter what comes against you, continue to look ahead for greater, for better. It's there, but we have to press forward. She encourages others to have the courage to spread their wings as eagles and fly, soar above obstacles and into the promises of God, knowing that God is truly the wind that is holding you up and keeping you up.

—S. Renee Brown